United States of America

United States of America

BY MICHAEL BURGAN

Enchantment of the World™
Second Series

CHILDREN'S PRESS®

An Imprint of Scholastic Inc.

New York   Toronto   London   Auckland   Sydney
Mexico City   New Delhi   Hong Kong
Danbury, Connecticut

Frontispiece: **Grand Canyon**

Consultant: James Wolfinger, PhD, Associate Professor, Department of History, DePaul University, Chicago, Illinois

Please note: All statistics are as up-to-date as possible at the time of publication.

Book production by The Design Lab

Library of Congress Cataloging-in-Publication Data
Burgan, Michael.
  United States of America / by Michael Burgan.
     pages cm.—(Enchantment of the world, second series)
  Includes bibliographical references and index.
  ISBN 978-0-531-23680-2 (lib. bdg.)
1. United States—Juvenile literature. I. Title.
  E178.3.B928 2013
  973—dc23   2013000084

1 2 3 4 5 6 7 8 9 10 R 23 22 21 20 19 18 17 16 15 14

University of Michigan marching band

Contents

Left to right: **Maine coast, Andy Warhol paintings, Taos Pueblo, President Barack Obama, farmworkers**

CHAPTER 1

A Nation of Immigrants

THE UNITED STATES IS A VAST COUNTRY, STRETCHING all the way across the North American continent and beyond. But whether Americans live near a sandy beach along the Pacific Ocean, on the plains and prairies of the Midwest, or along a rocky New England coast, they share many things. Many people enjoy a cookout on holidays. They enjoy watching a baseball game and exploring the country's natural wonders. But perhaps the most important thing they share is their pursuit of freedom.

Opposite: **The Statue of Liberty stands in New York Harbor. A symbol of freedom, it has greeted millions of immigrants arriving in their new home.**

The Growing Nation

Thousands of years ago, people first traveled to the continent of North America. They were the ancestors of today's Native Americans, who still live all across the nation. They were, in a sense, the first immigrants, people willing to leave their homelands and face uncertainty as they sought a new and better home. To some early European immigrants, the freedom of America meant being able to worship as they chose. For other immigrants, it meant working hard and making more money than they could in their homelands.

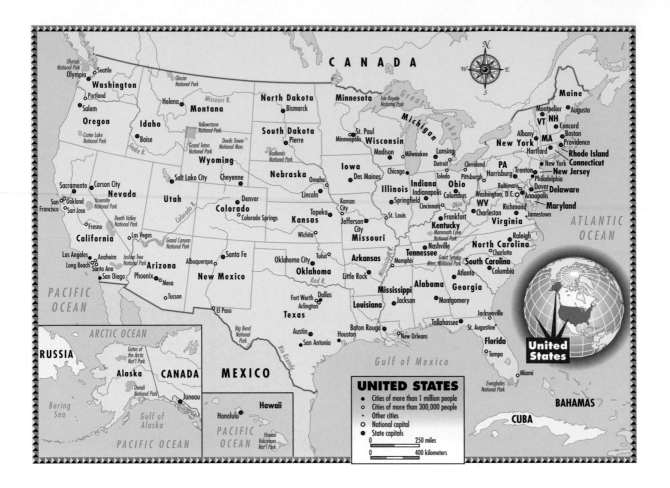

A land with abundant natural resources, the United States gave many settlers the chance to achieve success—whether through logging trees, mining gold, digging oil wells, or farming some of the richest soil in the world. Wealth and progress also came through technology. The United States has long been a country of great inventors, engineers, and scientists. The work of these people led to railroads that crisscrossed the nation and skyscrapers that rose over growing cities. Their creations included electronic devices to provide entertainment and computers that make the flow of information the fastest it has ever been.

The Struggles of a Nation

Today, the United States remains a nation of immigrants, home to people with roots in many different countries and with varied religious beliefs. The country's diverse citizens are united by the hope of building better lives for themselves and their children.

The unity of Americans has sometimes been tested. The Civil War divided the country over the issue of slavery. For many Americans, including enslaved African Americans and Native Americans who were forced off their lands, freedom has sometimes seemed distant. At times it was given only to those who were white or male or who owned property. The story of the United States has been one of slowly providing greater rights to all.

Slaves worked from sunup to sundown in the fields. At the beginning of the Civil War, there were four million enslaved people in the United States.

Despite their country's wealth, some Americans have struggled to find jobs and obtain access to health care and a good education. By the start of the twenty-first century, the United States seemed to be moving toward two extremes. At one end was a small number of people who were extremely wealthy and getting wealthier. At the other end, a great number of Americans were worrying about their future. Would there be good-paying jobs for them and their children? Would the United States maintain its position as the world's most powerful nation?

People stand in line to apply for jobs at the airport in Atlanta, Georgia. Currently, there are fewer jobs available for the middle class.

Land of Opportunity

Today, most Americans believe the country can overcome its problems. And people continue to come to the United States hoping to improve their lives. Each year hundreds of thousands of immigrants become U.S. citizens. Some are eager to vote in U.S. elections for the first time. Some hope to join the military and defend their new country. In 2012, Musu Jammeh, a native of Gambia, Africa, became a U.S. citizen. She was studying to be a nurse and had already learned much from her new country: "That's what America taught me. That if you work hard, you get opportunities, many opportunities." Americans hold on to this belief, even as they face challenges moving into the future.

New citizens say the Pledge of Allegiance for the first time as Americans. Each year, about five hundred thousand to one million people become U.S. citizens.

CHAPTER 2

From Sea to Shining Sea

THE MAINLAND UNITED STATES STRETCHES ABOUT 2,800 miles (4,500 kilometers) east to west across North America. It extends from the Atlantic Ocean to the Pacific Ocean, "from sea to shining sea," in the words of "America the Beautiful," one of Americans' favorite patriotic songs. Farther west, the states of Alaska and Hawaii are separate from the continental United States. The United States of America covers about 3.8 million square miles (9.8 million square kilometers) of territory, making it the third-largest country in the world. Only Russia and America's northern neighbor, Canada, are larger. Within this vast land are mountains and prairies, deserts, swamps, and forests that stretch as far as the eye can see.

Opposite: **Bass Harbor Head Light is in Acadia National Park, on Maine's rugged coast. Maine is the easternmost state in the country.**

Coastal Plain and Appalachian Highlands

The easternmost landform in the United States is the Atlantic Coastal Plain. It runs down the Atlantic coast and then curves westward along the Gulf of Mexico. This is a flat region, with the land gradually sloping down to the sea. In some places, such as Maine, the coast is rocky. In other places,

Geographic Features of the United States of America

Area: 3,794,101 square miles (9,826,676 sq km)

Highest Point: Denali (Mount McKinley), Alaska, 20,320 feet (6,194 m) above sea level

Lowest Point: Death Valley, California, 282 feet (86 m) below sea level

Longest River: Missouri, 2,540 miles (4,088 km) long

Largest Lake: Lake Superior, 31,700 square miles (82,100 sq km), shared with Canada

Largest State in Area: Alaska, 570,641 square miles (1,477,953 sq km)

Smallest State in Area: Rhode Island, 1,034 square miles (2,678 sq km)

Highest Recorded Temperature: Furnace Creek (Death Valley), California, 134°F (57°C) on July 13, 1913

Lowest Recorded Temperature: Prospect Creek Camp, Alaska, –80°F (–62°C) on January 23, 1975

Highest Average Annual Rainfall: Mt. Waialeale, Kauai, Hawaii, 486 inches (1,234 cm)

Lowest Average Annual Rainfall: Death Valley, California, less than 2 inches (5 cm)

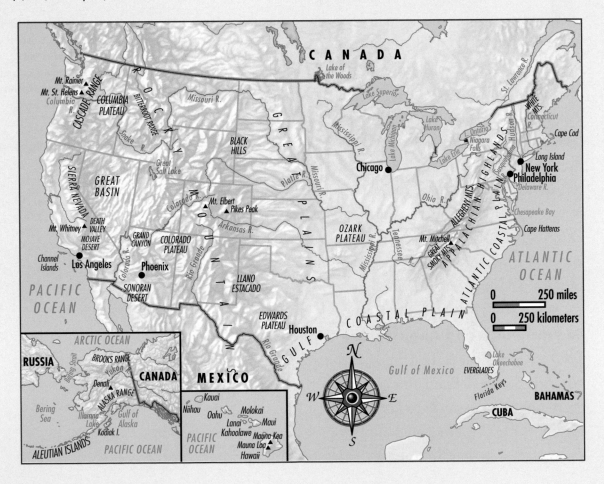

such as Louisiana and along the Chesapeake Bay in Maryland and Virginia, it is lined with swamps.

Just to the west of the Atlantic Coastal Plain are the Appalachian Highlands. The Appalachian mountain chain runs for almost 2,000 miles (3,200 km), from Alabama to Maine and then into Canada. Mount Mitchell, the highest peak in the Appalachians at almost 7,000 feet (2,100 meters), is in North Carolina. The Appalachian chain contains many mountain ranges, including the Great Smoky Mountains and the White Mountains. The Appalachian Highlands also include high, flat regions called plateaus. Great rivers such as the Hudson, the Susquehanna, and the Connecticut cut valleys through the highlands.

The Great Smoky Mountains lie along the border between Tennessee and North Carolina. They are named "Smoky" because they are often covered in fog.

Interior Plains

The Interior Plains cover the central part of the country. This region includes the flat lands of the Midwest and the Great Plains, which begin west of the Mississippi. Grass tall enough to hide a person on horseback once covered the central plains, which include what is now Illinois, Iowa, and Indiana. Today, that region produces such crops as corn and soybeans. Parts of the Interior Plains rise into mountains. South Dakota's Black Hills have peaks that reach above 7,000 feet (2,100 m). Mountains and plateaus rise in parts of Mississippi and Arkansas. Farther west, the Great Plains are flat in every direction, with farms and ranches covering the land.

The country's two longest rivers, the Missouri and the Mississippi, run through the Interior Plains. Other major rivers in the region include the Arkansas and the Platte. The

Exploring the Badlands

Badlands are areas of soft rock that has been eroded by wind and water. The creation of the landscape that is now at the heart of Badlands National Park in South Dakota began sixty-nine million years ago when a vast sea covered the region. When the sea dried up, it left behind sediment of clay and rock. Later rivers deposited more sediment. Then, starting about five hundred thousand years ago, new rivers cut through the region, wearing away the land to reveal colorful stripes of rock and carving striking towers of rock. Each year, a million people travel to western South Dakota to explore this extraordinary landscape.

country's largest lake, Superior, borders the northern region of the central plains. Lake Superior is one of the five Great Lakes, which stretch from Minnesota to northern New York.

Kayaking is popular along the shores of Lake Superior, the largest freshwater lake in the world.

Rocky Mountains and Colorado Plateau

The Rocky Mountains rise west of the Interior Plains. These towering mountains cut across the United States from Canada to central New Mexico. In Colorado, some peaks reach higher than 14,000 feet (4,300 m). The Colorado River and the Rio Grande cut through the southern Rockies. West of the mountain range is the Colorado Plateau, a region filled with canyons and dramatic rocks. The most famous of the canyons is Arizona's Grand Canyon, which was carved by the Colorado River several million years ago.

Pikes Peak

At 14,115 feet (4,302 m), Pikes Peak is not the tallest mountain in the Rockies, but to some Coloradans it's "America's Mountain." The peak is named for Zebulon Pike, an early American explorer in the region. In 1806, he led a small team of soldiers out of Missouri and west into the Rockies. His party tried to climb the mountain that now bears his name, but they weren't prepared for the wintry conditions they found and had to turn back. During their travels, Pike and his men went through five future U.S. states as well as part of Mexico. Pike died fighting the British during the War of 1812.

Great Basin and Columbia Plateau

West of the Rocky Mountains and the Colorado Plateau is the Great Basin, an area of alternating mountains and deserts. The deserts include the Sonoran Desert of southern Arizona and Mojave Desert of southeastern California. The mountains in this region sometimes reach higher than 5,000 feet (1,500 m).

North of the Great Basin, covering parts of Idaho, Washington, and Oregon, is the Columbia Plateau. Much of the land here was shaped by lava from volcanoes that erupted millions of years ago. Rivers in the region include the Columbia and the Snake. Some valleys in the Columbia Plateau have prime farmland, but other areas are too dry to support much agriculture.

Western Regions

The most westerly region of the continental United States is the Pacific Mountain System, which runs along the entire coast near the Pacific Ocean. A number of different ranges make up this system, including the Sierra Nevada and the Cascade Range. The Cascades are made up of many volcanoes. Some are still active. Mount St. Helens, in Washington State, erupted in 1980.

This region lies atop a boundary between two of the giant plates that make up the earth's outer layer. These plates are constantly moving in relation to each other, making these regions prone to volcanic activity and earthquakes. Many earthquakes have occurred along California's San Andreas Fault, and the city of San Francisco was badly damaged twice during the twentieth century.

The San Francisco earthquake of 1906 started many major fires. Together, the earthquake and fires destroyed more than 80 percent of the city.

The Pacific region is also home to much rich land. Valleys between California's coastal mountains and the Sierra Nevada have some of the world's best farmlands. Tall forests also line the coast.

The eastern part of Alaska, the largest state, borders Canada. The Rocky Mountains curve through part of Alaska after passing through Canada. Northern Alaska is mostly a flat, treeless landscape called tundra.

The most southerly part of the United States, Hawaii, lies about 2,400 miles (3,860 km) off the coast of California. Made up of a series of islands formed by volcanoes, Hawaii has tropical forests, beautiful beaches, warm waters, and mountains that reach almost 14,000 feet (4,300 m) high.

The Hawaiian Islands are filled with lush and rugged land. The Na Pali coast on the island of Kauai can be reached only by boat or on foot.

Great Cities

In 2011, nine U.S. cities had one million people or more. New York City, New York (right), with a population of 8.2 million, is the country's largest. It is home to immigrants from more than one hundred countries and is the financial and cultural center of the United States. Popular tourist sites include the Statue of Liberty, Times Square, and the Empire State Building.

Los Angeles, California, the second-largest city in the United States, has a population of 3.8 million. It was settled by the Spanish in the late eighteenth century, and today almost half its population has roots in Spanish-speaking lands. The city is home to Hollywood, the center of the U.S. movie industry. The music industry is also centered here.

Chicago, Illinois, is America's third-largest city, with 2.7 million residents. Located along Lake Michigan, it is known as the Windy City. It was once famous for its manufacturing and meat industries, but today is better known as the financial center of the Midwest. It is also famous for its architecture, with skyscrapers such as the Willis Tower (left, formerly known as the Sears Tower), which was once the tallest building in the world.

America's fourth-largest city, Houston, Texas, has a population of 2.1 million. It is named for Sam Houston, who helped Texas win its independence from Mexico in 1836. The city is home to many energy companies, a major port, and Mission Control for the U.S. space program, which coordinates all manned missions. Space Center Houston honors Houston's role in space exploration.

A boy snowboards off a picnic table in Minneapolis, Minnesota. An average of nearly 4 feet (1.2 m) of snow falls in the city each winter.

A Range of Climates

On a single day, the United States might see a blizzard in one place while in another location people are enjoying a warm, sunny afternoon. In general, the United States is said to have a temperate climate, meaning the weather varies over the four seasons. Summers are warm and winters are cold. But there is a great range within that broad climate pattern. Parts of California, for example, have what's called a Mediterranean climate, with hot, dry summers and wet, cool winters. Parts of Florida are considered tropical, with warm temperatures and higher humidity all year.

In general, temperatures are coldest in the northern parts of the country and warmest in the south. But even Alaska once saw the thermometer reach 100 degrees Fahrenheit (38 degrees Celsius). Rainfall tends to be low in the Great Basin and parts of the Great Plains and Rockies, but some mountain peaks in the Rockies get more than 300 inches (760 centimeters) of snow each year. Rainfall is generally heavier in the eastern part of the country and along the Pacific coast in Washington and Oregon.

The United States sometimes experiences extreme weather, with deadly effects. During 2012, about one-third of the country faced severe to extreme drought conditions. The worst-hit areas were in the Great Plains and the Southwest. The drought affected crops and led to damaging forest fires. Whirling storms called tornadoes sometimes strike the middle part of the country, causing sudden destruction. In 2013, massive tornadoes tore through Oklahoma. In Moore alone, more than twelve thousand homes were destroyed and twenty-four people were killed. The East is sometimes endangered by hurricanes. One of the worst ever, Katrina, hit along the Gulf Coast in 2005 and killed more than 1,800 people. Another powerful storm, named Sandy, struck the Northeast in 2012. Flooding damaged many coastal locations and shut down parts of New York City for days.

Warming Planet, Bigger Storms

In recent years, scientists have been tracking global warming—the rise in average global temperatures. This climate change has increased the frequency and severity of storms. Global warming is also melting the polar ice caps, which causes sea levels to rise. This means that when a hurricane reaches land it might push more water ashore in what is called a storm surge. Scientists predict that as the planet warms, storms will become more deadly.

CHAPTER 3

Wild and Wonderful

ALONG HIGH RIVER VALLEYS, BALD EAGLES SOAR above pine forests. On the coast of New England, seals come ashore on sandy beaches. In warm waters off Florida, sharks search for food. These animals and thousands of other kinds make their homes in the United States. Many different kinds of plants also thrive in the country. They range from mammoth redwood trees along the Pacific coast to tiny watermeals, the world's smallest flowering plants. Each one is barely the size of a pinhead!

Mammals

Each geographic region in the United States is home to a wide range of plants and animals. Some creatures can be found almost anywhere. Common mammals such as rabbits live in all fifty states. Other common small animals are squirrels and mice. Larger mammals include a variety of deer and their relatives, such as elk and moose. Elk are found mostly in the Rockies, while moose live in Alaska, some western states, and Maine.

Opposite: **Coast redwood trees, which grow only in northern California and southern Oregon, are the tallest living trees on earth. They often reach heights of more than 300 feet (90 m).**

Symbol of a Nation

The bald eagle is the symbol of the United States. To many people, it suggests courage, strength, and a sense of freedom. Bald eagles have a wingspan of up to 8 feet (2.4 m). Fish make up the largest part of their diet, but they also eat birds and mammals. The bald eagle was once common across the country, but by the 1960s, the number of mating pairs in the continental United States had fallen below five hundred. Many bald eagles had been hunted, while others were killed by pesticides—chemicals used to kill insects that harm crops. Thanks to government efforts, the number of bald eagles has rebounded, and this magnificent bird is no longer endangered.

The nation's wildcat population includes the Canadian lynx, which is found in the northern states; the bobcat, which is found almost everywhere except parts of the Midwest; and the mountain lion. Also called a puma, cougar, or panther, the mountain lion is found in the western part of the country.

Another big mammal is the bear. Bears will eat whatever they can find. Though they typically live in forests, in recent years, bears increasingly have been wandering into towns looking for food. During 2012, a severe drought around much of the country killed the wild food that bears usually eat. This forced more bears to search for food in areas populated by people.

Mammals also take to the sky and live in water. Forty-seven different types of bats live in the United States. In recent years, a disease called white-nose syndrome has killed more than five million bats in the eastern part of the country, and it seems to

be spreading. The disease is caused by a type of organism called a fungus. Water mammals include seals, dolphins, and whales. Many live in the waters off the U.S. coast during the warmer months and then move on as the cold sets in. Watching humpback whales rise out of the water, or breach, is a popular activity in Alaska and New England. Western humpbacks travel thousands of miles to reach warm Hawaiian waters in winter.

A grizzly bear catches a salmon in the Brooks River in Alaska. Fish are an important part of their diet.

Where the Buffalo Roam

The biggest of all U.S. land mammals is the American bison, or buffalo. A bison can weigh more than 2,000 pounds (900 kilograms) and stand 6 feet (2 m) tall at the shoulder. They are strong, powerful creatures, capable of running 40 miles per hour (65 kph). Tens of millions of bison once roamed across the Great Plains. They were hunted almost into extinction in the nineteenth century, and now only small herds live in the wild.

Fish, Reptiles, and Amphibians

Many different kinds of sea life live in the ocean along the U.S. coasts, including lobsters, crabs, and shrimp. Along the Atlantic coast, common fish species include cod and pollack. Whiting is a popular fish caught for food in the Pacific. Larger fish found in warm water include tuna, grouper, mackerel, and marlin. Inland, common fish in the west include salmon, while bass and trout can be found all across the country.

Water also provides a home for many kinds of reptiles and amphibians. The largest reptile in the United States is the American alligator, which sometimes grows 18 feet (5.5 m) long. This alligator, which lives in the southeastern part of the country, has a large mouth and can swim very fast. The gila monster,

About five million alligators live in the southeastern United States. Most are in Florida, Louisiana, and Georgia.

which lives in the desert in the Southwest, is one of the few poisonous lizards in the world. Dangerous snakes there include the poisonous rattler and water moccasin. More common and harmless are garter, hognose, and water snakes. In 2012, scientists in Florida studied the largest snake ever found in the United States, a Burmese python that was almost 18 feet (5.5 m) long. Pythons, though, are not native to the country. They first arrived as pets and then either escaped or were released into the wild.

Some of the most common amphibians found in the United States are turtles. The bog turtle, found along the East Coast, is only about 5 inches (13 cm) long. The alligator snapping turtle grows to about 26 inches (66 cm) long and weighs more than 150 pounds (70 kg). Leatherback sea turtles are even bigger, reaching up to 7 feet (2 m) long. They sometimes come ashore in Florida and along the Pacific coast. Other U.S. amphibians include frogs, toads, and salamanders. The largest frog, the bullfrog, is common in the East.

The Gila monster needs to eat only a few times a year. It eats small mammals, lizards, birds, and insects, but eggs are its favorite food.

Plant Life

A wide range of plants and trees live in the varied landscapes of the United States. Forests thrive in many parts of the country. In the northeast and the Appalachians are forests of pine, hemlock, spruce, and fir. Other eastern and southeastern forests include maple, oak, ash, and walnut. In swampy areas of the South, palmetto and cedar grow. In the mountains and plateaus of the West, the forests usually are dominated by pines or other cone-bearing trees. Fir, spruce, and redwood trees are all found in western forests.

High in the mountains of the West at elevations above 10,000 feet (3,000 m) is an ecosystem called alpine tundra. Few trees can grow in the cold alpine tundra. More common are shrubs, moss, and flowers adapted for the climate. For example, in the Rocky Mountains, some flowers have hairs on their leaves and stems to help protect them from cold winds. The blue columbine and some daisies are among the flowers that can survive in this region.

The desert of the Southwest is another extreme environment where flowers bloom. Cactuses and yucca plants can survive with little water, and they typically produce large, brilliant blooms. Other plants that can survive arid conditions include sagebrush and juniper, which are found in the Great Basin.

More than twenty thousand species of flowering plants are native to the United States. Others have been brought from overseas. Some wildflowers, like other wildlife, are threatened by human activity. Pollution or the spread of homes and businesses harm their habitats. Some of these increasingly rare flowers include the Florida skullcap, the Bear Valley sandwort of California, and the pitcher's thistle, found in the upper Midwest.

The pink blooms of a hedgehog cactus brighten the desert in Arizona's Organ Pipe Cactus National Monument.

CHAPTER 4

From Past to Present

THICK SHEETS OF ICE CALLED GLACIERS ONCE COVERED much of the earth. Between fifteen and twenty thousand years ago, so much of the world's water was bound up in ice that the sea level was lower. A broad swath of land between what are now Russia and Alaska was above water. This allowed settlers to walk from Asia to North America. From Alaska, they spread across the continent. Other early settlers may have used boats to reach North America. Regardless of how they arrived, their descendants became the first Americans.

These first settlers were hunters and gatherers. They used stone-tipped weapons to kill large elephant-like creatures, called mastodons, and other mammals. They also gathered wild fruits and nuts.

Indian Nations

About nine thousand years ago, people in Central America and Mexico began to settle down and raise crops, including corns, beans, and squash. Corn became a major crop for peo-

Opposite: **People have been living in Taos Pueblo in what is now New Mexico for about a thousand years. It is the oldest continuously occupied settlement in the United States.**

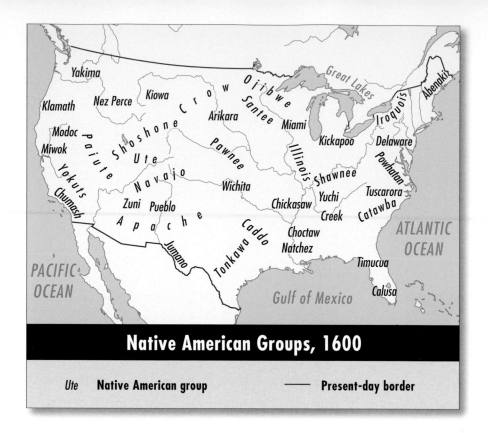

Native American Groups, 1600

Ute **Native American group**   —— **Present-day border**

ple across the Americas. Geography also shaped what people ate. Along the coasts and inland waters they relied on sea life. In desert regions of the Great Basin, some hunted and killed the reptiles that lived there.

Groups of native farming families built the first cities and complex societies in North America. Some of their cities housed several thousand people. Some of the largest were in the Southwest, where people used a mud-and-straw mixture called adobe to build homes. Native American nations traded with each other to acquire goods they did not have.

The Europeans Arrive

In 1492, Christopher Columbus, an Italian working for Spain, sailed from Europe and reached islands in the Caribbean Sea.

Mound Builders

In the Midwest and Southeast, some Native American groups built giant earthen mounds. People of the Mississippian culture built one of the largest of these mounds in Cahokia, in what is now Illinois. Monks Mound (left) is ten stories tall and covers 14 acres (6 hectares) of land. It was the center of a complex of 140 mounds. By 1100 CE, more than ten thousand people lived in Cahokia, and thousands more were in nearby villages. The city's leaders built their homes on the mounds, which were also used for religious ceremonies.

He made three more voyages to what Europeans called the New World. By the sixteenth century, explorers and soldiers from Spain reached various parts of what became the United States. Juan Ponce de León sailed from Puerto Rico to Florida in 1513. He returned several years later to try to start a colony, but the Calusa Indians of the region did not welcome the Spanish explorers. They drove off the Spaniards.

Over the next several decades, more Spanish explorers arrived. They sought riches, such as gold, and tried to start colonies. They also brought the first Africans to North America. Captured and forced into slavery, about one hundred Africans reached what is now South Carolina in 1526. The Spanish colony there failed, and some Africans stayed behind to live with local Native Americans. In 1565, Spain built a successful colony, St. Augustine, in Florida, making it the oldest European settlement in the United States. By the early 1600s, the Spanish also had a permanent colony in what is now New Mexico.

Searching for Gold

In 1539, reports reached Spanish officials in Mexico about "good and prosperous lands" to the north. The next year, Francisco Vásquez de Coronado led an expedition to find seven cities the Spanish thought were filled with gold. After months of trekking across Mexico and the American Southwest, Coronado's party reached the home of the Zuni people in what is now northern New Mexico. The expedition attacked the Native Americans. When they found no gold, Coronado and his group continued on, becoming the first Europeans to reach the plains of Kansas. They found no treasure there either. Discouraged, they returned to Mexico.

English and Dutch Settlements

Other Europeans also wanted to establish colonies in North America. The English tried to establish a colony in what is now North Carolina, but it failed. They had greater success with the Jamestown, Virginia, colony they founded in 1607. That colony almost failed, too, but with help from the Powhatan Indians the colony survived. At times, though, the English and Powhatan clashed. Tense relations continued for years. Eventually, the English outnumbered the Native Americans and forced them off their lands. That pattern repeated in following decades. The Native Americans tried to live with the European settlers, but the newcomers wanted their land and did not respect their way of life.

Farther north, along the Hudson River, the Dutch built several settlements. One of them, New Amsterdam, later became New York City. The Dutch called their colony New

Netherland, and they built a thriving fur trade with the local Native Americans. People from many European nations came to live and work there, some bringing enslaved Africans. The Dutch believed in religious freedom, and the first Jews to live in America reached their colony in 1654. In 1664, the English took over the Dutch lands, which became New York, New Jersey, and Delaware.

Meanwhile, to the northeast, the English had started another colony. In 1620, a group of people called the Pilgrims reached Plymouth, Massachusetts. A large group of Puritans reached the Boston area in 1630. They set up the Massachusetts

The Dutch traded metal tools, guns, and other items to Native Americans for furs.

Bay Colony. Both groups had left England because they objected to the practices of the Church of England and they wanted to practice their religion as they saw fit. The Puritans and Pilgrims shared some beliefs, such as following the Bible closely. Each colony based many of its laws on the Bible. They believed in working hard and making money in business. Success, they thought, meant God blessed them.

The English colonies grew as some Puritans and Pilgrims moved out of Massachusetts. They settled in Connecticut, Rhode Island, and the rest of what would become New England. North of Virginia, Roman Catholic settlers from England founded their own colony, called Maryland, in 1634. Tobacco became an important crop there, as it was in Virginia.

The owners of large farms, called plantations, had trouble finding enough workers to raise tobacco and other crops. The

Religious Freedom for All

Roger Williams was a Massachusetts Puritan who did not get along with local officials. He argued with them over politics and religion because he thought the two should be separate. After being forced out of Massachusetts, Williams started the neighboring colony of Providence in 1636, which later became the capital of Rhode Island. Unlike many colonists, Williams was respectful of the area's Native Americans, even learning their language. He also strongly believed in religious freedom. Rhode Island became a haven for Quakers, Jews, and other colonists who could not worship freely in other parts of New England.

farmers turned to indentured servants—poor people who agreed to work for seven years in return for their voyage to the colonies. The plantation owners also had to provide food, clothing, and shelter. By the end of the 1600s, the farmers relied more on enslaved Africans to do the work. Slavery became a main source of labor in the Chesapeake region and farther south, in the new colonies of North and South Carolina and Georgia. Slavery existed in every colony, but most slaves lived in the South. Meanwhile, northern merchants made money buying and selling slaves and providing food for large plantations.

Enslaved Africans were sold at auction. Families were often split up at these sales.

The Road to Revolution

By the middle of the eighteenth century, England was part of Great Britain, and the British had thirteen colonies along the Atlantic coast. Starting in 1754, Great Britain and France, which held lands to the north and west of the British colonies,

New Yorkers burn stamped papers in protest against the Stamp Act. The colonists were so hostile to the act that the British Parliament repealed it after only a few months.

fought the French and Indian War (1754–1763) for control of North America. The American colonists provided some troops and supplies, and the British won the war.

The war had been tremendously expensive, and the British wanted the American colonists to help pay for its cost and for the future defense of North America. The lawmakers in the British Parliament began passing taxes on the colonies to raise money. This angered many Americans. British citizens had members of Parliament representing them. Americans, however, did not have anyone representing their interests in Parliament.

Many colonists particularly disliked the Stamp Act, which placed a tax on most papers in the colonies, including legal documents, newspapers, and even playing cards. They violently protested against the act, especially in Boston. That city became the center of unrest against British policies that seemed to limit American rights. The British canceled the Stamp Act, but new taxes followed. As trouble brewed in Boston, King George III sent troops to keep order.

By 1773, Americans were still angry about the taxes, especially one on tea. In Boston, protesters disguised as Native Americans threw hundreds of crates of tea into the harbor. This "Boston Tea Party" angered King George, who called for new laws to restrict the rights of Massachusetts residents. More British troops arrived, the port of Boston was closed, and British officials took over local governments.

Many Americans couldn't stand to see Massachusetts denied its rights. They feared that their colonies might be next. In 1774, the colonists sent representatives to Philadelphia, Pennsylvania, for what was later called the First Continental Congress. The Americans asserted that they were loyal to the king, but that he and Parliament were wrong to take away their freedoms. But King George considered the Americans rebels. He would not back down.

American colonists hurl crates of tea into Boston Harbor during the Boston Tea Party. The colonists destroyed 342 chests of tea that night.

War for Independence

Some colonists, called Patriots, argued that America should become independent from Britain. In Massachusetts, many of them prepared for war. On April 19, 1775, British troops based in Boston headed into the countryside to destroy Patriot weapons and supplies. Along the way, they fought Patriot soldiers in Lexington and Concord. This is considered the first battle of the American Revolution.

Soon after, the Continental Congress named George Washington the commander of the American forces. Fighting went on outside of Boston, in New York and Virginia. In March 1776, the British left Boston, but they soon sent a larger force to New York City. In Philadelphia, Patriot leaders adopted the Declaration of Independence on July 4. Chiefly written by Thomas Jefferson of Virginia, the document said Americans were fighting for "life, liberty and the pursuit of happiness."

Sound the Alarm

Paul Revere of Boston is famous for his April 1775 midnight ride to warn Patriots that the British were on their way to attack. But sixteen-year-old Sybil Ludington also rode great distances to warn the Patriots about British military action. In April 1777, the British attacked Danbury, Connecticut. Sybil lived in a nearby New York town and her father commanded local troops known as militia. When word reached her father about the invasion, Sybil rode through the night to alert the militia to organize and fight. She had to dodge British troops in the area to carry out her mission. Sybil's ride did not make many history books, but today she is recognized for her bravery.

The war continued until the fall of 1781, when American soldiers and their French allies surrounded British forces at Yorktown, Virginia. The British surrendered on October 19. The Americans had won their independence.

Building a New Nation

During the American Revolution, U.S. leaders had created a national government with a document called the Articles of Confederation. Under this document, however, the government was too weak to collect taxes or build a strong nation. During the summer of 1787, leaders from every state except Rhode Island met in Philadelphia and created a new government, which they outlined in the Constitution. In 1789, George Washington was elected to serve as the first president of this new government.

During the country's early years, many issues divided Americans. One of the most important issues was slavery. Vermont outlawed slavery in 1777, and as time went on, more and more northerners began to oppose it. The southern states, though, still relied on slaves to grow tobacco, rice, and other crops. Meanwhile, Americans were moving westward, beyond the original thirteen states, into lands the country had won from Great Britain and bought from France.

George Washington became the leader of the Continental army in 1775 and led the American forces throughout the Revolutionary War.

The Louisiana Purchase

In 1803, France sold the United States a vast swath of land called the Louisiana Territory. For $15 million, Americans received 828,000 square miles (2,144,500 sq km) of land, stretching from the Mississippi River to the Rocky Mountains. This deal, called the Louisiana Purchase, just about doubled the size of the country and included land that made up all or most of thirteen future states. At the time of the purchase, the territory was home to about 50,000 people who traced their roots to Spain, France, and Africa, and about 150,000 Native Americans.

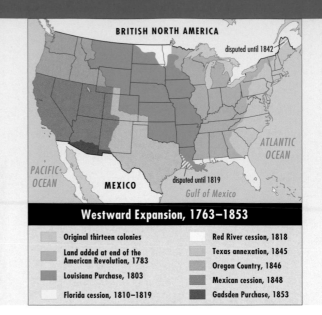

BRITISH NORTH AMERICA

disputed until 1842

ATLANTIC OCEAN

PACIFIC OCEAN

MEXICO

disputed until 1819

Gulf of Mexico

Westward Expansion, 1763–1853

- Original thirteen colonies
- Land added at end of the American Revolution, 1783
- Louisiana Purchase, 1803
- Florida cession, 1810–1819
- Red River cession, 1818
- Texas annexation, 1845
- Oregon Country, 1846
- Mexican cession, 1848
- Gadsden Purchase, 1853

Although Britain no longer ruled the United States, its actions still affected the country. In the early 1800s, Britain was at war with France, and in order to increase their number of troops, the British sometimes forced American sailors to join their navy. Americans grew angry with this practice, called impressment, and with British efforts to limit American trade. In June 1812, Congress declared war on Great Britain.

The War of 1812 lasted almost three years. Americans suffered losses on land as they tried to invade Canada. Meanwhile, in 1814 British troops marched on Washington, D.C., and burned much of the city. Most of the major U.S. victories came at sea. Although the war ended with no true victor, many Americans were satisfied with its outcome. They had showed European leaders they were ready to defend their rights and independence.

Decades of Growth

After the War of 1812, Americans looked forward to a bright future. The Industrial Revolution had begun. Factories producing cloth gave jobs to young women and children who once worked on farms. The government built canals to move people and goods more easily. Immigrants helped build the canals and then railroads, which first appeared in the United States around 1830. Some of the immigrants were Irish, who came looking for jobs after a famine struck their homeland in the 1840s. Germans had been coming to America since colonial days, and they continued to pour in. Many Irish and Germans settled in cities, while many immigrants from Scandinavia, in northern Europe, bought farmland in the Midwest and Great Plains.

Migrants walked 2,000 miles (3,200 km) across the country on the Oregon Trail. The journey from Missouri to the West Coast took four to six months.

Through these decades, the United States created new states. In 1845, Texas, then an independent country, joined the Union. The country gained more western lands by winning the Mexican-American War. The biggest prize was California. Gold was discovered there in 1848, and it fueled a gold rush. Miners raced there from around the world to seek their fortune.

America's wealth was growing, but so was the North–South split over slavery. As new states entered the Union, lawmakers had to decide whether slavery would be allowed in them. Slavery was legal, Southerners argued, so new states had a right to choose whether or not they wanted it. In the North, many people opposed the spread of slavery into new lands. Some wanted to outlaw it everywhere.

The *Dred Scott* Decision

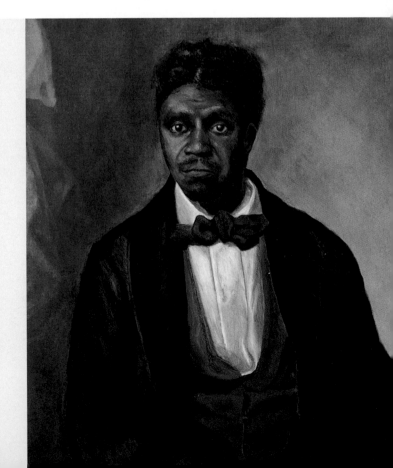

In the mid-1800s, an enslaved man named Dred Scott fought for his freedom in the courts. Scott's owner had taken him from the slave state of Missouri into free areas. Scott argued that the time he spent in a free state or territory made him free. Scott lost his case, which he appealed to the U.S. Supreme Court. The court ruled that Scott was still a slave. The justices went on to say that no African Americans, even free blacks, were citizens, and that the Constitution did not apply to them. The justices further ruled that Congress had no power to limit slavery in the territories. Slave owners welcomed the ruling and hoped it would end arguments over slavery. But antislavery groups were angry. The *Dred Scott* decision pushed the nation closer to war.

The Union and the Confederacy in 1863

- ⬛ Union state that outlawed slavery
- ⬛ Union state that allowed slavery
- ⬜ Union territory
- ⬜ Confederate state

The conflict reached a crisis point when Abraham Lincoln was elected president in 1860. Lincoln wanted to stop the spread of slavery into new areas, but he promised Southerners he would not end it in their states. Many Southern lawmakers, however, distrusted Lincoln. Following his election, Southern states started to secede from, or leave, the Union. By the following spring, eleven states had seceded. They formed a new country called the Confederate States of America. Lincoln said they had no legal right to secede. On April 12, 1861, Confederate troops fired on Union troops housed at Fort Sumter in South Carolina. The Civil War had begun.

Most of the fighting took place in the South. Tens of thousands of soliders died in the biggest battles, including Bull Run,

Antietam, and Shiloh. By the war's end, more than six hundred thousand soldiers were dead. In the end, the Union forces prevailed, as they had more money, more troops, and more supplies than the Confederates. After four years of fighting, Confederate general Robert E. Lee surrendered to Union general Ulysses S. Grant at Appomattox Court House, Virginia.

On April 14, 1865, just as the war was ending, a Southerner named John Wilkes Booth shot and killed Lincoln. Northerners mourned the loss of this great leader who had tried to keep the country together.

Still, the country had much work to do. It had to rebuild the South and address the rights of African Americans. The Thirteenth Amendment to the Constitution outlawed slavery. Other amendments made former slaves citizens and gave

Gettysburg

Gettysburg, Pennsylvania, was the site of the deadliest battle of the Civil War. Over three days in July 1863, about fifty-one thousand soldiers were killed, wounded, or went missing. The dead Union soldiers were buried at the site of the battle, and in November 1863, President Lincoln came to dedicate Soldiers' National Cemetery there. He gave a brief speech known as the Gettysburg Address, which is considered one of the greatest speeches in U.S. history. It closed with his promise that "government of the people, by the people, for the people, shall not perish from the earth." Today, the battlefield is part of Gettysburg National Military Park. Visitors can see items left behind on the battlefield, walk the field itself, and visit the graves of soldiers buried there.

black males the right to vote. But across the South, whites denied blacks their rights, often making it impossible for them to vote and keeping them out of schools and other public buildings whites used. This separation of the races, or segregation, was ruled legal by the U.S. Supreme Court in 1896.

Confederate general Robert E. Lee (far left) signed a document surrendering on April 9, 1865. Union general Ulysses S. Grant is seated at the right.

Rebuilding and Expanding

In many parts of the country, industries were growing. Steel plants rose in Pennsylvania and the Midwest, fueled by coal brought in on trains. Factories made farm equipment, canned foods, and items for the home, such as sewing machines. The work of millions of immigrants kept the country moving. Chinese and Japanese immigrants headed to the West Coast, while people from southern and eastern Europe came through New York and

Rights for Women

When the United States gained its independence, only men were allowed to vote. But in the mid-1800s, women such as Elizabeth Cady Stanton (right) and Susan B. Anthony began working to change the law. In 1869, Wyoming Territory granted women the right to vote. Other western states soon followed their lead. But change was slower in coming to the East. Many women could not vote until 1920, when the Nineteenth Amendment to the U.S. Constitution gave women the right to vote.

other eastern cities. Some Americans disliked these new immigrants. Workers claimed the immigrants took away their jobs. Others disliked the fact that many of the newcomers were not Protestant, as most Americans were at the time. By the 1880s, the country was setting up laws to keep out certain immigrants, and these laws would continue into the twentieth century.

The growth of industry meant some business owners grew very wealthy. Average workers, however, worked long hours for low wages. Some workers formed groups called unions to try to protect their interests. At times, the unions went on strike, or stopped working, to demand higher pay. Railroad strikes in 1877 and 1894 sparked violence.

At the beginning of the twentieth century, some American political leaders began arguing that the government should play a role in curbing the power of huge corporations and should help workers, the poor, and uneducated immigrants. They also wanted to give people more power in shaping laws and electing government officials. These reformers were known as Progressives.

Overseas Gains and Wars

As the nineteenth century was coming to an end, some Americans believed the nation should gain new lands overseas. Additionally, some U.S. politicians wanted to end European influence in North and South America. These goals came together in 1898, when the United States helped Cuba, an island in the Caribbean Sea about 90 miles (145 km) from Florida, in its fight for independence from Spain. During what is called the Spanish-American War, U.S. troops went to Cuba to help drive out the Spanish. Meanwhile, U.S. naval ships destroyed a Spanish fleet off the Philippines, another Spanish colony. When the war ended, the United States controlled the Philippines, Guam, and Puerto Rico. Cuba would soon be free. The same year, the United States took control of Hawaii.

Immigrants at Ellis Island wait for a ferry to New York City. In the late nineteenth and early twentieth centuries, about twelve million immigrants passed through Ellis Island.

In 1914, World War I began in Europe. U.S. president Woodrow Wilson wanted to stay out of the war. However, he favored France and Great Britain—the Allies—against their main enemy, Germany. The United States sent supplies to the Allies. In 1917, Germany began using submarines to attack all commerical ships headed to Great Britain. Wilson responded by saying that the United States must join the Allies against Germany. The war ended the following year with a German surrender.

Highs and Lows

After the war, the country entered an era called the Roaring Twenties. The war was over, and people were ready to move on. More and more people bought cars, telephones, and household

Nearly five million American troops fought in World War I. More than one hundred thousand of them were killed.

appliances, and businesses prospered. But even as the country seemed to be doing well, there were signs of trouble ahead. Farmers were producing more crops than people could buy, so prices began to fall, reducing farmers' profits. Factories also were producing more goods than they could sell, so some companies began firing workers. Finally, in October 1929, the prices of many stocks, shares of the ownership of a corporation, began to fall. Banks asked investors to pay back loans they had taken to buy stocks, but many investors didn't have the cash. The value of stocks fell even more, and soon the country was in its worst economic crisis ever, the Great Depression.

By 1933, about 25 percent of Americans were out of work. Many had lost all their savings when banks went out of business. In 1932, Franklin Roosevelt won the presidency, promising Americans a "New Deal" to soften the effects of the Depression. The government would become more active than ever before in shaping the economy and helping the needy.

During World War II, so many men were in the military that many factories began hiring women for the first time. Here, a female worker inspects bomb casings at a plant in Nebraska.

Under Roosevelt, the government hired people to build roads and bridges. The elderly began to receive Social Security money to help pay their bills. The government also built dams to create electricity in rural areas. These programs and others helped people survive. But the Depression itself did not end until World War II began. American factories began to hum as they manufactured weapons and other military supplies.

Becoming a World Power

In 1939, Germany invaded Poland. Germany's ally Japan had already invaded China. Together with Italy, Germany and Japan were known as the Axis powers. They sought to use their military might to take over foreign lands. Opposing the Axis powers were Great Britain, France, and later, the Soviet Union (a large nation made up of Russia and other nearby countries). They were known as the Allies. Roosevelt supported the Allies, but he knew most Americans wanted to stay out of another world war.

On December 7, 1941, Japan launched a surprise attack on the U.S. military base at Pearl Harbor, Hawaii. As a result, the United States joined the war, fighting in Asia, North Africa, and Europe. Slowly, the Allies pushed the Japanese off islands Japan had taken in the beginning of the war. The Allies began to use these islands as bases to attack Japan. In Europe, General Dwight D. Eisenhower commanded an invasion of France, to take back land Germany had captured early in the war.

In May 1945, Germany finally surrendered. Japan surrendered in August, after the Americans dropped an atomic bomb on the city of Hiroshima and, soon after, another on Nagasaki. These bombs were the most powerful weapons ever made. In Hiroshima, the single bomb killed at least 130,000 people that day.

When the war ended, the United States had the world's strongest economy and strongest military. It would take the lead in rebuilding nations damaged by the war.

Cold War Decades

In the years after World War II, conflict grew between the United States and the Soviet Union. The Soviet Union was a Communist country. Under this system, the government owns most businesses and controls the economy. One political party controls all of society. Many Americans feared that the Soviets were spreading Communism around the world. Starting with President Harry Truman, U.S. presidents were determined to stop Communism from spreading. The struggle between the United States and the Soviet Union is known as the Cold War.

The conflict was called "cold" because the two countries did not fight each other directly. Countries each side supported sometimes fought, though, and those countries received military aid from the two superpowers. The Korean War (1950–1953) and the Vietnam War (1954–1975) were the major examples of this. In both cases, U.S. troops fought in Asia to try to stop the spread of Communism. The Korean War ended with Korea split in two, one-half Communist and one-half democratic. The Vietnam War ended with the Communists controlling the whole country.

The greatest fear of the Cold War years was that the two superpowers would start a nuclear war. In 1949, the Soviets tested their own atomic bomb. Then, U.S. and Soviet scientists raced to develop more powerful bombs and rockets that could carry

The Cuban Missile Crisis

The worst crisis of the Cold War came in 1962. A new government in the island nation of Cuba was seeking aid from the Soviet Union and let the Soviets base nuclear missiles in Cuba. Cuba sits just 90 miles (145 km) south of Florida, and the missiles could have hit most major cities in the United States. President John F. Kennedy went on nationwide television to announce that he had told the Soviet Union to remove the missiles. For a few tense days, no one knew if the crisis would result in a nuclear war. Finally, the Soviets agreed to remove their missiles from Cuba, while Kennedy promised not to attack Cuba in the future and to remove from the nation of Turkey U.S. missiles that were aimed at the Soviet Union.

the bombs thousands of miles. By the early 1960s, the two countries had enough nuclear weapons to kill hundreds of millions of people. Beginning in the late 1960s, leaders of the two nations held talks to reduce the number of weapons. Finally, in 1991, the Soviet government collapsed, ending the Cold War.

Turbulent Times

The American economy boomed during the Cold War years, as workers made military equipment, cars, and household goods. Government loans made it easier for returning soldiers to buy homes and go to college. But some people were left out of the country's growing wealth. African Americans, in particular, still faced segregation and were often kept from voting and getting good jobs. In the 1950s, many brave people joined peaceful marches, strikes, and sit-ins to try to force an end to segregation. They struggled and sometimes died in the fight to gain equal rights and treatment for blacks throughout the country.

In 1960, African Americans began staging sit-ins at lunch counters that refused to serve them. Their peaceful protests were covered in the news and raised awareness around the country of the growing civil rights movement.

I Have a Dream

In the 1950s and 1960s, Martin Luther King Jr. (1929–1968) was the most prominent voice of the civil rights movement. A minister from Atlanta, Georgia, he took part in marches across the South to bring an end to the discrimination African Americans experienced in all aspects of their lives. He believed in nonviolence, even when white police officers beat peaceful protesters. In 1963, King gave one of the most famous speeches in U.S. history. In his "I Have a Dream" speech, he said he looked forward to the day when all Americans would "not be judged by the color of their skin but by the content of their character." King was murdered on April 4, 1968, in Memphis, Tennessee.

The 1960s was a turbulent time in America. Many young people wanted to change the country. They held massive protests, demanding that the U.S. government bring American soldiers home from Vietnam. By the time the Vietnam War ended in 1975, fifty-eight thousand U.S. soldiers had died.

Meanwhile, women, Hispanics, and Native Americans all demanded better treatment. They too wanted equality.

Recent Times

By the late 1970s, some Americans were arguing for a different kind of change. They wanted to reduce the role of government in society. In 1980, Ronald Reagan won the presidency promising such a change. He said, "Government is not the solution to our problem; government is the problem." He and his supporters wanted lower taxes and less spending on programs that helped the poor.

Yet no one denied the government's role in defending U.S. citizens. That role came into focus on September 11, 2001, when members of a terrorist group called al-Qaeda flew planes into the World Trade Center skyscrapers in New York City, and into the Pentagon, the country's chief military building, near Washington, D.C. Another plane crashed in Pennsylvania before it could hit its target. Almost three

On September 11, 2001, terrorists crashed two jets into the twin towers of the World Trade Center in New York City. Both towers soon collapsed.

thousand people died that day, and President George W. Bush promised to strike back against al-Qaeda. He sent troops to Afghanistan, where al-Qaeda's leaders were hiding out.

Then, in 2003, Bush sent a larger force into Iraq. He said Iraq was helping terrorists and trying to build nuclear weapons. Iraq had no ties to the September 11 attacks, and it was eventually confirmed that the country did not have nuclear or biological weapons. However, the United States forced Iraq's dictator Saddam Hussein from power, and U.S. troops remained there until 2011.

U.S. forces invaded Iraq in March 2003. American troops remained in Iraq until 2011.

In 2008, the United States made history when it elected Barack Obama, the first African American president. Obama took over a country facing its worst economic crisis since the Great Depression. Some members of Congress resisted his efforts to spend money to keep people working, but he was able to loan money to two of the three major U.S. car companies so they could stay in business. Additionally, he made plans to end the U.S military role in Afghanistan.

Entering his second term in 2013, Obama led a nation sharply divided over politics and how to strengthen its economy. But most Americans still believe they live in the greatest country in the world, a wealthy, powerful nation that attracts people seeking freedom and democracy.

Barack Obama took the oath of office to become the forty-fourth president on January 20, 2009. Prior to becoming president, he had been a senator from Illinois.

From Past to Present **63**

CHAPTER 5

Government
of the
People

N January 2013, Barack Obama stood in front of the nation and was sworn in as president for the second time. Like every president before him, he made an oath, or promise, to defend the Constitution of the United States. The Constitution spells out how the national government is set up and its relation to the states. The U.S. system is known as a federal government, since power is shared among the national (also called federal) government, the states, and the people themselves.

Over the years, Americans have sometimes changed the Constitution, adding amendments. The first ten amendments, added in 1791, are called the Bill of Rights. They guarantee that all Americans have a right to free speech, to worship as they choose, and to a fair trial, among other rights. Changing the Constitution is not easy. A proposed amendment must be passed by two-thirds of each house of Congress and then by three-quarters of the states. The leaders who wrote the Constitution wanted to make sure Americans thought carefully and took time before they made changes to their basic political document.

Opposite: **The Army's Old Guard Fife and Drum Corps, dressed in colonial clothing, marches past the Capitol during the presidential inauguration in 2009. The corps has marched in presidential inaugurations since 1961, including Obama's second inauguration in 2013.**

The Branches of Government

The U.S. Constitution reflects the idea of the separation of powers. This means that governmental power is divided among three branches of government. State and local governments also have this separation of powers. The Constitution promotes the idea of checks and balances. Each federal branch has rights and duties that help it check the powers of the other two. In this way, no one branch dominates the government.

National Anthem

"The Star-Spangled Banner" is the national anthem of the United States. A lawyer named Francis Scott Key wrote the lyrics after he saw the British navy bombard Fort McHenry in Baltimore, Maryland, during the War of 1812. The music comes from a popular British song. It was adopted as the nation's official national anthem in 1931.

Oh, say can you see by the dawn's early light,
What so proudly we hailed at the twilight's last gleaming?
Whose broad stripes and bright stars thro' the perilous fight,
O'er the ramparts we watched, were so gallantly streaming?
And the rockets' red glare, the bombs bursting in air,
Gave proof thro' the night that our flag was still there.
Oh say, does that star-spangled banner yet wave
O'er the land of the free and the home of the brave?

The U.S. Capitol includes a dramatic domed room filled with statues of prominent Americans.

The Legislative Branch

The legislative branch proposes and shapes laws for the United States. The country has 535 lawmakers, with 435 in the U.S. House of Representatives and 100 in the U.S. Senate. Together, these two lawmaking bodies are known as the U.S. Congress. Each state elects two senators, while the number of representatives is based on a state's population, with every state guaranteed at least one representative. On average, each member of the House represents 725,519 people, who together form a district. Representatives serve two-year terms, while senators serve six-year terms.

Congress has several specific duties. Only the House of Representatives can write bills, or proposed laws, dealing with taxes. For a bill to become a law, both houses of Congress must pass the bill. It then goes to the president, who can either sign it into law or veto (reject) it. Congress can overturn, or override, a veto, if two-thirds of the members of each house vote to do so.

Seeking Statehood

For decades, some people in Washington, D.C., and Puerto Rico have wanted these regions to become states. Residents of both areas are U.S. citizens, and in each region voters elect a representative to the U.S. House, but this person cannot vote on bills. Neither region is represented by anyone in the U.S. Senate. Unlike Puerto Ricans, Washington residents get to vote for president. The first time a majority of Puerto Ricans said they would like their island to be a state was in 2012. The decision, though, is up to Congress, not the people of Puerto Rico.

The Senate must ratify, or approve, treaties with foreign nations. It must also approve the people chosen by the president for certain government positions, such as the heads of departments. Congress has the sole power to declare war against a foreign nation. It can also remove certain government officials from office if they commit crimes, a process called impeachment. In recent decades, Presidents Richard Nixon and Bill Clinton faced the impeachment process. Nixon resigned, while Clinton was found not guilty of the charges brought against him.

President Richard Nixon, surrounded by his family, gives the nation his farewell address after resigning in August 1974. His vice president, Gerald Ford, became president.

The Executive Branch

The executive branch carries out the laws of the country. The executive branch includes the offices of the president and vice president, the departments under the president's control, and several independent agencies. These agencies include the National Science Foundation, which gives money for scien-

The National Aeronautics and Space Administration (NASA) is one of the many independent agencies in the federal government. Here, NASA engineers celebrate the successful landing of the *Curiosity* rover on Mars.

tific research, and the Central Intelligence Agency, which gathers information about other countries.

The president is the leader of the executive branch. To be elected president, a person must have been born in the United States and be at least thirty-five years old. A president cannot serve more than two four-year terms in office. If the president dies or cannot carry out the duties of the office, the vice president takes over as president.

U.S. voters do not directly elect the president and vice president. Instead, they are chosen by a body called the Electoral College. Each state has as many electoral votes as the number of representatives and senators it has in Congress. Candidates must receive a majority of the electoral votes to be elected president. In a few cases, one candidate has received the most popular votes across the country, but not enough electoral votes to win. This happened most recently in 2000, when George W. Bush won the presidency, even though his opponent, Al Gore, had received half a million more popular votes than Bush had.

The president of the United States is the head of the government and the head of state. He or she has many important duties. The president names people, called ambassadors, to represent the United States in foreign countries and appoints judges to federal courts. The Senate must approve these choices. The president is also the commander in chief. In that role, the president directs the military during times of war.

The U.S. government currently has fifteen executive departments. Each one focuses on a specific area of government service, such as defense, justice, agriculture, and education.

First Lady and More

Before becoming First Lady of the United States, Hillary Clinton (1947–) worked as a lawyer and was First Lady of Arkansas when her husband, Bill Clinton, was governor of the state. The Clintons came to Washington, D.C., in 1992 when Bill Clinton was elected president. As his term was coming to an end in 2000, Hillary won a seat in the U.S. Senate, making her the first former First Lady to hold such a high office. In 2008, she ran for president but lost. She then became secretary of state for President Barack Obama, until 2013. In that role, she traveled the world, representing American interests with foreign nations. Clinton became one of the most respected women in the country.

Red, White, and Blue

The flag of the United States of America was created during the American Revolution. By most accounts, Francis Hopkinson of New Jersey receives credit for designing the flag in 1777. Some people claim Betsy Ross sewed the first flag, but many historians doubt this, though she did sew flags flown on Pennsylvania ships. The original flag had thirteen alternating red and white stripes and a blue patch in the upper-left corner with thirteen white stars. The thirteen stripes stood for the thirteen states that won American independence from Great Britain. Over time, one star was added to the flag

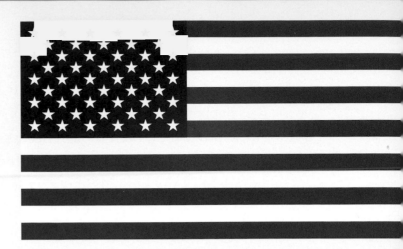

for each new state joining the Union. Today's flag still has thirteen stripes, along with fifty stars.

The head of each department is appointed by the president, and together those people form what is called the cabinet. The cabinet advises the president on important issues.

President Barack Obama consults with General Lloyd Austin. As commander in chief, the president is deeply involved in military affairs.

National Government of the United States

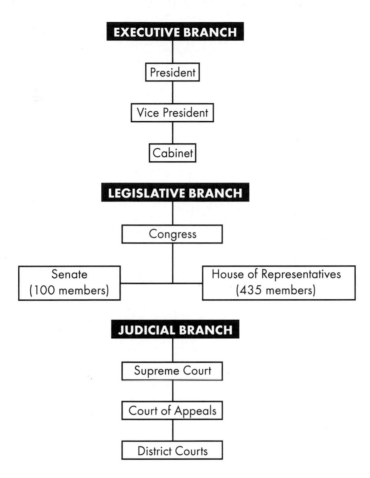

EXECUTIVE BRANCH

President

Vice President

Cabinet

LEGISLATIVE BRANCH

Congress

Senate
(100 members)

House of Representatives
(435 members)

JUDICIAL BRANCH

Supreme Court

Court of Appeals

District Courts

Judicial Branch

The federal judiciary has several different levels. Trials involving federal laws are held in the nation's ninety-four district courts. A decision in a district court can be appealed to one of the thirteen courts of appeals. The nation's highest court is the U.S. Supreme Court, which has nine justices. Supreme Court justices, like all federal judges, are appointed for life by the president. The

Supreme Court reviews cases that have been tried in other federal courts. It can also review cases that began in state courts if the cases involve constitutional issues. The Supreme Court has the power to decide if a state or federal law violates the Constitution. A law ruled unconstitutional can no longer be enforced.

The federal judiciary also has a number of separate courts that deal with specific legal issues. These include courts for deciding tax laws and appeals made by members of the military.

John Roberts, the chief justice of the Supreme Court, walks with Sonia Sotomayor, the court's first Hispanic justice, after she was sworn in in 2009.

State and Local Government

Every U.S. state has its own government that is similar in structure to the federal government. Each state has a constitution and three branches of government. A state executive branch is led by a governor. Like the U.S. president, governors can approve or veto laws and appoint certain officials. The judicial branch can have various levels of courts, with a state supreme court at the top. The state legislatures pass laws for that state. Every state except Nebraska has a legislature with two houses. State legislators usually serve either two- or four-year terms.

Below the state government comes the county government. In most states, counties have some sort of elected executive official and county board. Counties often have their own court systems also. The duties of county governments include building and maintaining schools, roads, and hospitals.

Members of the Virginia legislature discuss a law to ban smoking in many workplaces. State legislatures make laws that affect only their states.

Michael Bloomberg was mayor of New York City from 2002 until 2013. The founder of Bloomberg L.P., a financial data and media company, he is also a successful businessperson.

City and town governments have many different forms. Larger cities usually have mayors and a city council. In some cases, the mayor has great power to name department heads and propose new developments. Some cities and towns have a manager instead of a mayor. The manager is a hired official who carries out the orders of the council.

Political Parties

The United States has two major political parties, the Republican and the Democratic. Smaller parties include the Libertarian and Green, and candidates can also run independently of any party. Democrats tend to support using the federal government to solve such problems as poverty and pollution. Republicans, on the other hand, typically favor business and want to keep taxes low.

The Nation's Capital

In the years during and after the American Revolution, several different cities served as the capital of the United States. In 1800, Washington, D.C., became the permanent capital. *D.C.* stands for District of Columbia, the name given to land taken from Maryland and Virginia to form the capital region. (Virginia received back its share in 1846.) The city's main waterway is the Potomac River, which separates the capital from Virginia, to the west. Maryland borders the city on its other sides.

The three branches of the government are based in Washington, D.C., along with most executive departments. It is also where the president lives, in the White House. The city is famous for its landmarks honoring past presidents, such as the Lincoln Memorial, the Jefferson Memorial, and the Washington Monument. Other sites honor veterans killed in World War II, Korea, and

Vietnam. The Smithsonian Institution operates a series of museums, including the National Air and Space Museum (above), the National Museum of the American Indian, and the National Museum of American History.

Washington, D.C.

CHAPTER 6

Making a Living

Since the time of the earliest English colonies, America has given newcomers the chance to make a new life for themselves. Both before and after independence, America offered people the chance to buy land cheaply, find jobs, and start their own businesses. In the early years, many people made their livings in farming, fishing, the lumber industry, and trade. Today, many people provide services ranging from driving buses to creating software for computers to investing money for others. Millions of Americans, however, still produce goods in factories, raise crops, and fish. The work of all Americans, no matter what their jobs, contributes to giving the United States the largest economy in the world. The nation's gross domestic product (GDP)—the total value of goods and services it produces—was about $16 trillion in 2012.

Opposite: **A farmer monitors the corn coming out of a harvesting machine. About 80 percent of the corn grown in the United States goes into animal feed.**

Making a Living **79**

Money Matters

U.S. currency comes both in paper bills and metal coins. The fronts of both kinds of currency feature historic figures, while the backs often show important buildings or symbols of the nation. All currency produced in the United States has the phrase "In God We Trust" on it. Coins also have the Latin saying *E Pluribus Unum*, "out of many, one." Here are the bills and coins commonly used in the United States, with the name of the person who appears on them:

Penny (1 cent)	Abraham Lincoln
Nickel (5 cents)	Thomas Jefferson
Dime (10 cents)	Franklin D. Roosevelt
Quarter (25 cents)	George Washington
Half-dollar (50 cents)	John F. Kennedy
$1 bill	George Washington
$5 bill	Abraham Lincoln
$10 bill	Alexander Hamilton
$20 bill	Andrew Jackson
$50 bill	Ulysses S. Grant
$100 bill	Benjamin Franklin

Living off the Land

Agriculture was a major source of food for many native people who lived in North America when Europeans first arrived there. It remained the main source of income for most Americans for several hundred years. As rich farming areas in the Midwest and California were settled, large farms became common.

Farming today is big business, though less than 1 percent of the population makes a living in agriculture. The United States is the world's second-largest producer of agricultural products, having recently been passed by China. America produces more barley, oats, soybeans, and peanuts than any other country. The country also exports, or sells overseas, more corn and wheat than any other nation. The United States is ranked number one in the production of beef and poultry and is a major producer of cotton, pork, apples, and much more.

California is the nation's largest producer of agricultural goods. Almost half of the country's fruits, vegetables, and nuts come from there. Its climate is perfect for growing crops found almost nowhere else in the country, such as almonds, dates, and walnuts. California also produces more milk and cream than any other state.

After California, the next largest agricultural producers in 2011 were Iowa, Texas, Nebraska, and Illinois. Iowa is the nation's top producer of corn, followed by Illinois. Those two states also lead in producing soybeans. Texas grows more cotton than any other state. It also raises the most cattle for beef. Nebraska, though, is number one in the amount of total red meat produced.

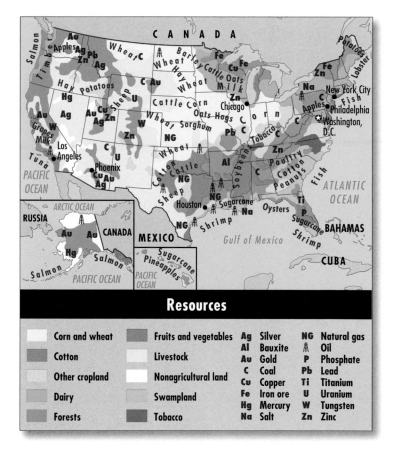

Manufacturing and Mining

Once, steel mills and factories were common across the United States. Today, about 20 percent of Americans work in industry, construction, or transportation. That's down from almost 50 percent during the middle of the twentieth century.

The Big Apple

A company that started in a California garage during the 1970s grew into one of the most valuable corporations in the world. It 2012 it was worth more than $600 billion. That company is Apple, which Steve Jobs founded with his friend Steve Wozniak. Jobs became the public face of the company, which offered such popular products as the iPod for music and the iPad for computing on the go. Jobs wanted Apple products to look as good as they performed, and people were willing to pay more for those products than the ones other companies offered. Jobs became a hero to people who admired his attention to detail and his efforts to win loyal customers. In a commencement speech in 2005, Jobs gave the graduating class advice that he had followed throughout his successful career: "Your work is going to fill a large part of your life, and the only way to be truly satisfied is to do what you believe is great work. And the only way to do great work is to love what you do." Jobs died of cancer in 2011 at age fifty-six.

Manufacturing remains important to the U.S. economy. The country manufactures a huge range of products, including electronics, clothing, medicines, automobiles, and heavy equipment, such as the kind used in construction or on farms. The United States is home to one of the world's top airplane makers, Boeing.

The United States has extensive mineral resources. It is the world's third-largest oil producer and is a major producer of natural gas and coal. Large amounts of copper, iron, lead, magnesium, and zinc are also mined in the United States.

What the United States Grows, Makes, and Mines

AGRICULTURE (VALUE OF PRODUCTION, 2010)

Corn	$66,650,000,000
Soybeans	$38,915,000,000
Hay	$14,401,000,000

MANUFACTURING (SALES, 2010)

Petroleum and coal products	$1 trillion
Computers and other electronic products	$581 billion
Chemicals	$387 billion

MINING

Hard coal (2007)	506,351,000 metric tons
Oil (2007)	1,847,000,000 barrels
Copper (2009)	1,190,000 metric tons

Services

The service sector is the largest part of the U.S. economy, employing almost 80 percent of all workers. Service jobs include selling goods in stores, providing insurance or financial information, or managing people in offices. Education, government service, and jobs related to tourism are also part of the service sector.

Many Americans work in the computer industry. They write the software used to run computers and the applications used for online social media. Facebook, which was founded on a U.S. university campus, now links more than one billion people around the world. Microsoft, once the top software company in the world, now battles with Google and other companies in that field.

Measuring Up

For weighing and measuring most products, the United States uses a system first brought to North America by English colonists, now called the customary system of measurement. Distance measurements include the inch, the foot (12 inches), the yard (3 feet), and the mile (5,280 feet). For weighing objects, the common measurements are the ounce, the pound (16 ounces), and the ton (2,000 pounds). Liquids are measured using the ounce, the pint (16 ounces), the quart (32 ounces), and the gallon (128 ounces). In 1988, Congress passed a law calling the metric system the preferred system of weights and measures. This system is based on units of 10. For example, the basic measure for distance is the meter. One thousand meters equals a kilometer. Despite Congress's actions, few Americans, except scientists and engineers, use the metric system.

One of the biggest service industries is health care. In 2010, more than fourteen million health care professionals played some role in keeping people healthy. They work at universities doing research or in hospitals and doctors' offices. Some provide care in nursing homes or inside patients' houses. Doctors treat the sick with high-tech tools, such as digital scanners and robotic surgery systems. The United States leads the world in making these kinds of complex devices.

Transportation

Transportation-related industries make up about 10 percent of the country's GDP. Trucks, trains, ships, and planes all move goods. Major airports include Chicago's O'Hare and Atlanta's

Hartsfield-Jackson. The country's busiest ports for handling large containers of goods are Long Beach and Los Angeles, both in California. The United States has just over 4 million miles (6.4 million km) of paved roads and more than 140,000 miles (225,000 km) of railways.

A jet takes off from Los Angeles International Airport in California. It is the third-busiest airport in the country, with more than thirty million passengers passing through every year.

CHAPTER 7

Many People, One Nation

SHORTLY AFTER AMERICA'S FOUNDERS DECLARED independence in 1776, they set to work creating a great seal for the new country. This seal would represent what the United States stood for. When the seal was finally approved six years later, it contained the Latin phrase, *E Pluribus Unum*. This means, "out of many, one." The separate colonies had come together as new states to form the Union. And within those states, people from different backgrounds came together to run the government and build the nation. The tradition of blending many peoples into one united country continued with each wave of immigration to the country. That process still goes on today.

Opposite: **Children attend a Flag Day parade in New York City.**

Today's Immigrants

The United States has great cultural diversity. About 40 million of the nation's estimated 314 million residents in 2012 were born in a foreign country. These immigrants made up about 13 percent of the population. Most came from Latin America and Asia, with Mexico being the most common country of birth.

Leading Home Countries of U.S. Immigrants	
Mexico	19.3%
China	8.6%
India	7.7%
Philippines	4.1%
Korea	3.2%
Cuba	2.8%
Dominican Republic	2.7%
Vietnam	2.4%
El Salvador	2.0%

The immigrants include refugees, people fleeing war or harsh political rule in their homelands. The United States has always welcomed refugees. Before and after World War II, refugees came from Europe. Many Americans originally from Vietnam and other Southeast Asian countries came to the United States after the Vietnam War. Today, Iraq is the source of most refugees, as that country still struggles to rebuild after the U.S. invasion of 2003. A plaque at the Statue of Liberty, erected in 1886, says that the country welcomes those "yearning to breathe free." That's still true today.

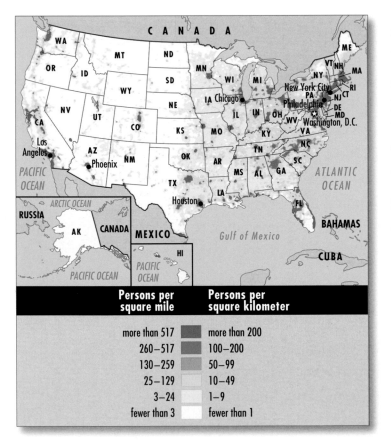

Persons per square mile	Persons per square kilometer
more than 517	more than 200
260–517	100–200
130–259	50–99
25–129	10–49
3–24	1–9
fewer than 3	fewer than 1

City and Country

Where do the several hundred millions of Americans live? Most of them—84 percent—live in larger towns and cities. The number of people living in less populated rural areas has fallen dramatically over the past century. In 1910, 72 percent of the country lived in those small towns and villages.

Today, the state with the largest population is California, with more than thirty-seven million people. At the bottom of the list is Wyoming, with fewer than six hundred thousand people. Other

largely rural states include Vermont, North and South Dakota, and Montana. New Jersey is the most densely populated state. It has an average of 1,189 people living in each square mile (459 per sq km). Alaska, the largest state in size, has just 1.3 people per square mile (0.5 per sq km).

Population of Largest Cities (2011 est.)	
New York City, New York	8,244,910
Los Angeles, California	3,819,702
Chicago, Illinois	2,707,120
Houston, Texas	2,145,146
Philadelphia, Pennsylvania	1,536,471
Phoenix, Arizona	1,469,471
San Antonio, Texas	1,359,758
San Diego, California	1,326,179
Dallas, Texas	1,223,229
San Jose, California	967,487

A Hispanic teenager gives his little brother a ride. New Mexico has a higher percentage of Hispanic residents than any other state, at 46 percent.

Race and Ethnicity

The United States has an increasingly diverse population. People with roots in Europe make up the largest part of the country's population. Today, most Americans of European background trace their roots to Germany, Great Britain, Ireland, Italy, Poland, and Scandinavia. The percentage of Americans of European descent is dropping. In 2011, more than half the babies born in the country were nonwhite.

The fastest-growing part of the population is Hispanic or Latino, people whose roots are in Spanish-speaking countries.

About 16.3 percent of the people in the United States are Latino. In recent years, many Latinos have moved to the South and the Midwest. But just three states—Florida, California, and Texas—are home to more than half the nation's Latinos. People with Mexican roots make up the largest Hispanic group, but many also have Puerto Rican or Cuban backgrounds. An increasing number of Hispanic immigrants are coming from El Salvador, the Dominican Republic, and Guatemala.

African American and Asian American populations are also growing. The number of blacks grew more than 12 per-

Racial Identity (2010)

White	72.4%
Black/ African American	12.6%
Asian	4.8%
Native American/ Alaska Native	0.9%
Native Hawaiian/ Pacific Islander	0.2%
Other race	6.2%
Two or more races	2.9%

Interracial marriages are becoming much more common in the United States. Fifteen percent of all marriages that took place in 2010 were between people of different races.

cent between 2000 and 2010, faster than the population as a whole. A growing number of Americans also have a mixed racial background of African roots combined with one or more other races. More than 50 percent of African Americans live in the South, though several northern cities have large black populations. New York is home to more African Americans than any other state.

Revelers shoot confetti into the air to celebrate Chinese New Year. About 3.8 million people in the United States trace their ancestry to China.

Illegal Immigration

Among the forty million foreign-born Americans, about ten million entered the country without the legal right to do so. The presence of illegal immigrants angers some Americans, who believe these immigrants take jobs from legal residents or use government services they shouldn't receive. Some Americans also believe that since the immigrants broke the law when they entered the country, they should be sent back to their homelands. Others, however, argue that the immigrants often do difficult work, such as picking crops, that most Americans don't want to do. The immigrants also pay taxes. Some Americans support amnesty—letting people who are already here stay in the country and giving them the chance to become citizens.

The population of Asian Americans increased 43 percent between 2000 and 2010. Much of this growth came from immigration. More Asians live in California than in any other state. People with Chinese, Indian, Filipino, Vietnamese, and Korean backgrounds make up the largest groups. A growing number of people identify themselves as both Asian and another race.

The Native American population has remained small over the decades. Native Americans are scattered across the country, though California, Oklahoma, and Arizona have the most. Oklahoma is home to many Cherokees, which is the nation's largest Native American group. The second-largest nation, the Navajo or Diné, is centered in Arizona and New Mexico. Alaska has the highest percentage of residents with Native American heritage, at almost 20 percent.

Most Common Languages Spoken at Home After English (2009)

Language	Number of Speakers
Spanish	35.4 million
Chinese	2.6 million
Tagalog (Filipino language)	1.5 million
French	1.3 million
Vietnamese	1.2 million
German	1.1 million
Korean	1.0 million
Russian	880,000
Arabic	850,000

Language

The United States does not have an official language, though English is the one most commonly spoken. In immigrant communities, newcomers often speak their native language. The children of immigrants usually learn English quickly, while still sometimes also speaking the language of their parents.

Keeping Languages Alive

At the time Europeans first arrived in the land that would become the United States, the native people already living there spoke more than 300 different languages. As Europeans spread across the continent, many Native American nations disappeared, their languages lost. Only about 175 Native American languages are still spoken in the country today, and many of those have only a few elderly speakers still using them. In 2006, Congress passed a law that gave Native Americans money so they could teach their children their own languages.

A Jewish boy reads in Hebrew at his bar mitzvah, a coming-of-age ritual that takes place at age thirteen.

About 20 percent of Americans are bilingual, with Spanish being the most common second language.

Many immigrant communities publish newspapers in their native languages. Some also set up schools. In New Jersey, a number of private schools teach Indian immigrants Hindi, the most common language of India. Arab and Jewish parents sometimes have their children learn the languages used in their religious services: for Jews, Hebrew, and for Muslims, Arabic. And on many Native American reservations, children learn the languages of their ancestors.

CHAPTER 8

Spiritual Life

WHO OR WHAT CREATED THE UNIVERSE? WHAT happens to people after they die? Since the beginning of humanity, people around the world have turned to religion to help answer such questions. Native Americans formed their own religious beliefs. Europeans brought Christianity and Judaism to the colonies. Later immigrants arrived with faiths such as Islam, Buddhism, and others. Overall, the United States remains a religious country, much more so than most European countries.

Native Religions

The first people in North America told stories to explain how the world was created. Each Native American group developed its own religion. Though these religions vary, they typically include a variety of spirits that control nature and parts of human life. Some Native American religious ceremonies include dances to honor the spirits, while others feature masks or dolls believed to have spiritual power. In some

Opposite: **About three-quarters of Americans are Christian.**

Religion in the United States (2007)	
Protestant	51.3%
Roman Catholic	23.9%
Jewish	1.7%
Mormon	1.7%
Buddhist	0.7%
Jehovah's Witness	0.7%
Muslim	0.6%
Orthodox Christian	0.6%
Hindu	0.4%
Other	1.5%
Unaffiliated	16.1%
Did not answer	0.8%

Creating the World

Every culture has its own creation story. Here's one from the Cherokee people.

The animals lived in the sky above a large body of water. As the sky got crowded, a water beetle went down to explore what was below the water. The beetle found mud, which it brought up to the surface. The mud began to spread out across the water, creating the earth. The ground was soft, and a huge buzzard that flew down to explore the earth created hills and valleys by flapping its wings into the mud. The mud finally dried, and the animals came down to live on earth.

Native American religions, spiritual leaders called shamans are believed to be able to contact the spirit world and receive important information from the spirits.

As Europeans settled in America, they often tried to force Native Americans to give up their beliefs and instead practice Christianity. In Spanish-speaking areas, native people often blended their beliefs with the Spaniards' Roman Catholicism. At times, some Native Americans continued to practice their religion secretly, while outwardly appearing to accept Christianity.

Protestants in America

The first Christian faith to reach what became the United States was Roman Catholicism. Catholic priests arrived in Florida with Spanish explorers during the 1560s.

In the thirteen colonies, Protestantism was the main religion. Many early American colonists were Puritans and Pilgrims, who wanted to break away from or reform the Church of England. By the time of the American Revolution, Protestants in America included Methodists, Congregationalists, Baptists, Lutherans, Dutch and German Reformed believers, Presbyterians, Quakers, and members of smaller churches, most of which still exist. Today, the largest single Protestant denomination, or group, is the Southern Baptist Church. The second largest is the United Methodist Church.

There are many different branches of Protestantism, with varying beliefs. Evangelicals believe they can save their souls through faith in Jesus Christ, whom they consider to be the son of God. They also believe it is their duty to try to convince others to accept Jesus. Pentecostals believe that God acts directly through certain people. For example, some people might receive from God the power to heal the sick without using medicine.

John Winthrop

John Winthrop was a lawyer who played a key role in bringing Puritans and their faith to America. He was deeply religious and wanted the freedom to practice his Puritan beliefs and spread them in the new colonies. In 1630, he led about one thousand Puritans from Britain to Massachusetts. Before landing in America, Winthrop spoke about the importance of what the immigrants were doing. He said the new Puritan community would be "a city upon a hill." The world would be watching to see if the Puritans could honor God and succeed in America. Since then, many Americans have used Winthrop's phrase to mean that the United States is a model for other nations to follow.

The Church of Jesus Christ of Latter-Day Saints, also known as Mormonism, is a Protestant-based faith that developed in the United States in the 1830s. Mormonism is one of the fastest-growing faiths in the world. In 2012, Republican Mitt Romney became the first Mormon to run for president as the candidate of a major party. He brought increased attention to the church.

Catholicism and Orthodox Christianity

Although Spaniards were the first people to bring Roman Catholicism to America, later immigrants from Ireland, Italy, and other nations helped make Roman Catholicism the largest Christian denomination in the United States. More recently, Hispanic immigrants have also boosted church membership. The church is based in Vatican City, in Italy, and is led by the pope.

Home for a New Religion

During the 1840s, Mormons traveled west to Utah from the Midwest so they could practice their faith as they chose. Under the leadership of Brigham Young, they built a huge temple. Made to look like a European church, with tall, pointed spires, the temple took forty years to complete. The Salt Lake Temple (right) remains the largest Mormon temple in the world. Next to it is the dome-shaped tabernacle, home of one of the world's largest pipe organs and the Mormon Tabernacle Choir. The sound inside is so good, a person in the back of the building can hear a pin dropping to the floor at the front of the tabernacle.

Native American Saint

During the seventeenth century, French priests brought Roman Catholic teachings to what is now upstate New York. A young Mohawk woman named Kateri Tekakwitha (1656–1680) decided to become a Catholic and then went to Canada to spread Catholicism there. After she died, some people reported seeing visions of her, and a few years ago, the Catholic Church said she had been responsible for healing a very sick boy. In 2012, the Church named Tekakwitha a saint, an exceptionally holy person. She is the first Native American saint.

Almost a thousand years ago, the Christian Church split, creating the Roman Catholic Church and the Orthodox Church. The Orthodox Church later split into separate churches based in different countries. In the United States, immigrants from eastern Europe, Greece, and the Middle East brought the Orthodox

Catholics attend a mass at the Cathedral of Our Lady of the Angels in Los Angeles.

faith to America. The first were Russians who settled in Alaska during the 1790s. Today, the Greek Orthodox Church is the largest Orthodox denomination in the United States.

Judaism and Islam

The first Jews in America came from Spain and Portugal. Starting in the 1840s, many came from Germany. Then, later that century, most came from eastern Europe and Russia. Today, Judaism has several different denominations, including Orthodox, Conservative, and Reform.

Islam is now the fastest-growing religion in the United States. Muslims believe that in the seventh century CE, God revealed messages to Muhammad. Muhammad spread these messages, starting the new religion of Islam. Islam has many ties to Christianity and Judaism. Muslims believe in the Bible, but they consider Jesus a prophet rather than the son of God.

Between 2000 to 2010, the number of Muslims in the United States increased by almost 67 percent. Some Muslims are immigrants, while others have converted from other religions. A 2007 poll found that most Americans who converted to Islam had been Protestant, and more than half were African American.

Other Religions

Buddhism first came to America with Japanese immigrants. Today, people from many Asian nations, including Thailand, Tibet, and Vietnam, pray at Buddhist temples in the United States. Many Americans have converted to the faith as well. Buddhists follow the teachings of the Buddha, who lived in

India more than 2,500 years ago. Buddhists do not believe he was a god, but that he created a system of thought and action that could improve people's lives.

Hinduism is the main religion of India, and many immigrants from there and other Asian countries practice that faith in America. Hindus believe that when people die, they are reborn, or reincarnated, as new living beings.

Some Americans don't attend a particular church or follow one religion's teachings. A growing number of Americans say they don't believe in God or practice any faith. Since the 1970s, some people have embraced New Age beliefs or spirituality. This sometimes combines Asian and European religions with Native American ideas. Thanks to the Constitution, Americans have the freedom to worship as they choose, and the freedom to choose not to worship at all.

A Muslim woman in Dearborn, Michigan, plays with her son. The Qur'an, the holy book of Islam, says that Muslims should dress modestly, and some women follow this by covering their hair and neck.

CHAPTER 9

Creating Culture

WALK DOWN A STREET IN LOS ANGELES, California, and you might see a painting on the side of a building. Search the Internet, and you can come across short films people made in their own homes. Music plays in stores. In theaters across the nation, actors take to the stage to sing, dance, tell jokes, or tell stories of their lives.

In the United States, art is all around. It is sometimes labeled serious, such as paintings found in museums or the classical music played in concert halls. Art also includes popular culture, which can be anything from comic books to TV shows. Folk art ranges from Native American jewelry to the wood carvings of a farmer in Vermont.

Art

The earliest examples of art found in what is now the United States are carvings on rocks made by native people. These petroglyphs are common in the Southwest and can also be found in

Opposite: **A musician plays a melodica, an instrument that combines a woodwind and a keyboard.**

Pennsylvania, Michigan, and other states. Traditionally, Native Americans also made goods that were both useful and beautiful. They made colorful pottery, masks and dolls used in religious ceremonies, reed baskets, clothing decorated with porcupine quills, and giant carved wooden totem poles.

With the arrival of Europeans, the arts in America changed, though slowly. The first settlers had to focus on building homes, clearing fields, and raising crops. But by the eighteenth century, the first great American artists emerged. Most painted portraits of other people, though some showed scenes from the country's early history. John Singleton Copley, Gilbert Stuart, Charles Willson Peale, and John Trumbull are some of these early painters.

The Hudson River School art movement emerged in the early nineteenth century. Painters such as Thomas Cole and Frederic Church painted large, colorful scenes of the Hudson River valley and other natural spots in the Northeast. Many American artists studied in Europe. Some, such as Mary Cassatt, lived there for many years. Cassatt studied a type of painting called impressionism, in which artists try to capture the light and their perception of the subject rather than painting exactly what something looks like. Cassatt became renowned for her paintings of women and children.

During the twentieth century, many artists tried to express the fast pace of the modern world and the belief that art could be whatever they said it was. A movement out of New York called abstract expressionism captured some of those ideas. One of the greatest abstract expressionists, Jackson Pollock,

Georgia O'Keeffe

Georgia O'Keeffe (1887–1986) made a name for herself creating large paintings of flowers and other objects extremely close up. People praised the intimacy and vitality of the paintings. In 1917, O'Keeffe visited New Mexico for the first time. She was mesmerized by the stark landscape. O'Keeffe visited the region often and moved there permanently in 1946. She devoted much of the rest of her life to capturing the landscape on canvas. Over and over, she painted the cliffs, the sky, and the sun-bleached bones of cattle that had died in the arid land. O'Keeffe is considered one of the greatest American painters of the twentieth century.

Andy Warhol painted *Campbell's Soup Cans* (partial, below) in 1962. It included thirty-two paintings, one each of every kind of soup Campbell's produced at the time.

dripped and hurled paint onto canvases set on the floor, creating paintings bursting with energy. By the 1960s, some artists were making everyday objects the subject of their work, in a style called pop art. Andy Warhol became famous for making exact paintings of Campbell's soup cans. In the 1980s, the work of graffiti artists such as Keith Haring moved from the street into galleries and museums.

Photography and Architecture

Photography was developed in the nineteenth century, and many early photographers tried to capture daily life. Others, such as Mathew Brady, who took thousands of pictures of Civil War scenes, became chroniclers of early American history. By the twentieth century, the work of photographers such as Alfred Stieglitz, Ansel Adams, and Edward Weston ensured that photography was considered an art form. More recently, Cindy Sherman earned acclaim for her work, which often features portraits of herself dressed as different people.

Thomas Jefferson was one of the great early architects in the United States. He was influenced by European styles when he designed his Virginia home, Monticello. Frederick Law Olmsted was a landscape architect, who designed huge parks, such as New York's Central Park. Toward the end of the nineteenth century,

In Cindy Sherman's work, she dresses up as different characters and then photographs herself.

In 1935, Frank Lloyd Wright designed Fallingwater, a house that extends over a waterfall in Pennsylvania. Fallingwater is renowned for fitting in perfectly with its surroundings.

Louis Sullivan and Daniel Burnham helped create some of the world's first skyscrapers in Chicago, Illinois. One of the nation's most influential architects, Frank Lloyd Wright, favored simple, geometric shapes and low, flat buildings. In recent years, I. M. Pei has been among the nation's leading architects. Pei makes elegant, geometric buildings such as the Rock and Roll Hall of Fame in Cleveland, Ohio. Frank Gehry, another leading architect, designs exuberant buildings often covered in metal, such as the Walt Disney Concert Hall in Los Angeles.

Literature

Writing has been important in America since the colonies were first established. Ministers wrote sermons, and many people wrote letters and kept diaries. America's first publishers printed Bibles, and by the early 1700s, newspapers appeared. Histories of the colonies, poetry, and plays were also written.

American literature exploded in the nineteenth century. Nathaniel Hawthorne wrote dark tales about Puritan New England in books such as *The Scarlet Letter*, while Herman Melville is remembered for his epic tale of a whale, *Moby-Dick*. Mark Twain mixed humor and morality in books such as *The Adventures of Tom Sawyer* and *The Adventures of Huckleberry Finn*, and is considered one of America's greatest writers. The nineteenth century also saw the rise of many great poets, such as Emily Dickinson and Walt Whitman.

Major writers of the mid-twentieth century include Ernest Hemingway, William Faulkner, and Saul Bellow. They each

Writing for Teens

Fiction for young adults has surged in popularity in recent years. One of the most successful young adult authors is Suzanne Collins, who wrote *The Hunger Games* trilogy. In these books, teens from a frightening future must fight in a game for their survival. They must kill other children like themselves or be killed. The books are wildly popular. As of 2012, Collins had sold more books on Amazon's Kindle e-reader than any other author.

won the Nobel Prize in Literature, the world's highest honor for a writer. More recently, Toni Morrison was the first African American woman to win the Nobel Prize. Her vivid novels, which include *Song of Solomon* and *Beloved*, explore the lives of African Americans.

Buster Keaton in a scene from *The Cameraman*, made in 1928. Keaton was a master of physical comedy.

Film

Since the early 1900s, the center of the film industry has been Hollywood, California. American films have played around the world and become part of international culture. From the silent comedies of Buster Keaton to the wartime romance of *Casablanca* to epic fantasies such as *Star Wars*, American films have captured the imagination of the world. Many Hollywood actors have also won worldwide fame. Some of the best in recent years include Johnny Depp, George Clooney, and Matt Damon. Meryl Streep, whose career began in the 1970s, is one of the most respected American actors today. As of 2013, she had been nominated for seventeen Academy Awards, the highest honor in the film industry, and won three.

Meryl Streep won her third Academy Award for the 2011 film *The Iron Lady*. She has been nominated for more Oscars than any other actor.

Music

Music was important to traditional Native American life and was often used in religious ceremonies. The most common instruments were voices, drums, and rattles. As other people arrived in America, they brought with them different influences that shaped the music heard throughout the land. The Scots-Irish who settled in the South helped create bluegrass music, which has a fast tempo and features the mandolin, fiddle, banjo, and guitar. Folk music from the British Isles

Jazz has many different styles. Saxophonist Charlie Parker (center) led in the development of bebop, a style that features fast tempos, complex harmonies, and long improvisations.

influenced folk music and country music that developed in America. Today's stars of country music include Taylor Swift, Blake Shelton, and Carrie Underwood. Settlers from across Europe brought classical music, and in recent times notable American composers have added to this field. They include Aaron Copland, Leonard Bernstein, and Philip Glass. Immigrants from Spanish-speaking lands, especially Mexico, Puerto Rico, and Cuba, brought such musical forms as salsa and mariachi.

African Americans have been central in forging new types of music. Uniquely American music includes gospel, which was originally sung in black churches, and the blues, which developed from songs slaves sang as they worked. Elements of both shaped rhythm and blues. Jazz also blended elements of earlier black musical forms. Its creativity and complexity helped make it popular around the world. Some of the greatest jazz musicians of all time were Louis Armstrong, Charlie Parker, and Miles Davis.

Starting in the 1950s, black musical styles combined with country music to create rock and roll. Some of the great early American rock performers were Buddy Holly and Jimi Hendrix. Bob Dylan has often blended rock and folk music with poetic lyrics, making him one of the greatest songwriters the country has produced.

Hip-hop is a more recent African American musical form that has been embraced around the world. Top hip-hop artists of recent years include Kanye West, Jay-Z, and Nicki Minaj.

Beyoncé

Beyoncé Knowles (1981–) first earned fame in the 1990s as part of the group Destiny's Child. The group, which performed rhythm and blues and hip-hop, was one of the most popular acts of the decade. After leaving the band, Beyoncé was usually known only by her first name. She became renowned for her vocal range and power. She has released several albums that won many Grammy Awards, the highest honor in the U.S. music industry, and is considered one of the most influential musicians in the world. Beyoncé has also branched out into acting, starring in such films as *Cadillac Records* and *Dreamgirls*.

CHAPTER 10

Daily Life

ON A TYPICAL DAY, AMERICANS WAKE UP AT vastly different times. When a Hawaiian rolls out of bed at 7:00 a.m., it's already 9:00 a.m. in California and noon in New York. The different time zones reflect the size of the country. Across this large country, the lives of individual Americans vary greatly. A person who runs a large company might own several lavish homes, while hundreds of thousands of people have no homes at all and are forced to spend the night in shelters or huddled on the street. Between these two extremes fall the vast majority of Americans.

From Home to Work

People in the United States talk about the American Dream, and part of that dream is owning a home. In 2010, about two-thirds of all Americans lived in their own home. A large number of

What to Wear

Americans wear a huge variety of clothing. Men and women who work in offices often wear suits. Students at some private schools are required to wear uniforms. But the piece of clothing most associated with the United States is blue jeans. These pants, made out of a rugged material called denim, were first developed in California during the gold rush of the nineteenth century. Cowboys wore them, then sailors, and then movie stars and musicians. By the 1960s they were a symbol of American youth. People like them because they are durable and comfortable.

Americans choose to live in suburbs, mainly residential towns that surround larger cities. But in recent years, cities have seen larger population growth than suburbs. Many young people are choosing to stay in cities, and some elderly people are moving back to them to be close to shopping and cultural events.

When Americans leave their homes to go to work or go shopping, they're likely to do it in a car. Americans own about 254 million cars for personal use. Many Americans also use mass transit to get to work. Across the country, more and more rail systems are being built, enabling people to live outside a city and not have to drive to get to work. But many people can only reach their jobs by driving. Some people choose to live in isolated areas, so they can have privacy or be close to nature. Others are forced to drive long distances because they can't find work where they live. The number of people driving 90 miles (145 km) each way to and from work is on the rise. It might take these people ninety minutes or more to get from home to work.

Education

In 2012, the United States was home to about 75.6 million students at all levels of schools, from elementary to college. Most children in the United States attend public school. About 8 percent attend private schools, many of which are religious.

Computers are common in American classrooms.

On the Road

In the United States, each state sets speed limits for its roads. In the Northeast, the top speed on highways is 65 miles per hour (105 kph). Farther west, in states that are predominantly flat and rural, the top speed limits are 70, 75, or 80 miles per hour (113, 121, or 129 kph). The state with the highest speed limit in the nation is Texas. In 2012, it increased the speed limit on a 41-mile (66 km) stretch of a major highway to 85 miles per hour (137 kph)!

Carnegie Libraries

During the late nineteenth and early twentieth centuries, many American towns built their first public libraries thanks to Andrew Carnegie. A Scottish immigrant, Carnegie made a huge fortune in the steel industry. For a time, he was the richest man in the world. Although he went to school for only three years, he loved to read and knew the value of education. Starting in the 1880s, he donated $40 million to build more than 1,600 libraries across the country. Many of these Carnegie libraries are still operating.

After high school, many students go on to college. Admission into the best schools in the country is extremely competitive. About 40 percent of America's students earn a college degree. Students typically take four to six years to earn their degree. College in the United States is often very expen-

Students relax outside at Harvard University in Cambridge, Massachusetts. Founded in 1636, Harvard is the oldest university in the United States.

sive. In 2009, the average annual tuition at public universities, which are funded by the government, was more than $7,000 a year. That doesn't include food, housing, books, supplies, or other expenses. At some private universities, a year's tuition is $50,000. Many students take out loans to attend college.

Food from many parts of the world is now popular throughout the United States. Indian food is one type that is commonly found in train stations and shopping malls.

Time to Eat

American food combines elements of many different countries. Immigrants to the United States brought their foods with them, and now American food might mean a pizza, with roots in Italy, or a taco, originally from Mexico. Asian, Middle Eastern, African, and Caribbean restaurants can be found in large cities and increasingly in suburbs and towns as well. According to a 2011 survey, the most popular ethnic cuisines that people eat out are Italian, Mexican, Chinese, pan-Asian, and Japanese.

On some special occasions, Americans of all backgrounds eat a common meal. On Thanksgiving, turkey is the center of

As American as Apple Pie

People have been eating apple pie in America since colonial times. Long ago, it was a common breakfast food. Today, it is more often a dessert. Here's a simple recipe for apple pie you can make with an adult.

Ingredients

2 9-inch pie crusts

¼ cup all-purpose flour

¾ cup granulated sugar

½ teaspoon ground cinnamon

½ teaspoon ground nutmeg

Dash of salt

6 cups thinly sliced apples

2 tablespoons butter

Directions

Preheat the oven to 425°F. Mix together the flour, sugar, cinnamon, nutmeg, and salt in a large bowl. Stir in the apples. Place one crust on the bottom of a pie pan. Dot the crust with butter. Add the apple mixture, and then cover with the top crust. Make small slits in the top crust to let steam escape. Seal the top crust to the bottom crust by pinching the edges together. Bake 40 to 50 minutes, until the crust is brown and juice begins to bubble through the top. Enjoy!

National Holidays

New Year's Day	January 1
Martin Luther King Jr. Day	Third Monday in January
Presidents' Day	Third Monday in February
Memorial Day	Last Monday in May
Independence Day	July 4
Labor Day	First Monday in September
Columbus Day	Second Monday in October
Veterans Day	November 11
Thanksgiving	Fourth Thursday in November
Christmas	December 25

the meal. During the summer, holidays such as the Fourth of July call for a barbecue or picnic. Hamburgers and hot dogs cooked on the grill and potato salad, cole slaw, and other salads are popular for those celebrations.

A young boy celebrates the Fourth of July by eating a hot dog.

Having Fun

Americans, like people the world over, want time to relax and enjoy themselves. In the United States, people can pursue their leisure activities at home, at parks and beaches, and inside sporting arenas. One popular activity is watching TV. On an average day, the typical adult watches more than two hours of television.

Girls roller skate through Golden Gate Park in San Francisco, California.

Teens and the elderly watch slightly more. Many people also like to play video games. Almost half the homes in America have a device that is strictly for playing video games. Video games aren't just for kids—the average player is thirty years old.

Sports are wildly popular in the United States. Baseball is called the national pastime, and its championship, the World Series, has been played since 1903. Basketball was invented in Springfield, Massachusetts, in 1891, and is now one of the most popular sports around the world. American football draws fans to stadiums that can hold up to one hundred thousand people. Soccer is the most popular sport around the world, but professional soccer has struggled to gain wide appeal in the United States. The sport is very popular, however, with young people and with immigrants. During the late twentieth century, auto racing

The New York Giants run onto the field before a game. According to polls, football is the most popular sport in the United States.

Millions of people visit American amusement parks every year. Roller coasters are among the biggest attractions.

became one of the most popular spectator sports in America. The National Association of Stock Car Auto Racing (NASCAR) began in the South and then spread across the country.

Americans also enjoy traveling during their leisure time. They visit cities, explore natural wonders, and camp out in some of the country's national parks. The National Park Service controls almost four hundred areas set aside for their natural beauty or historic importance. The most visited is the Great Smoky Mountains National Park in North Carolina and Tennessee. Other popular vacation spots include Orlando, Florida, which is home to several large amusement parks; Washington, D.C., which is filled with monuments and museums; and New York City, which has an abundance of art and entertainment.

Wherever they go and whatever they do, Americans have many choices for how to live their lives. The freedom to choose and to live as one wants is what drew so many people to the country initially. The United States will keep attracting newcomers, as long as it offers freedom and the chance to build a better life.

IN THIS TEMPLE
AS IN THE HEARTS OF THE PEOPLE
FOR WHOM HE SAVED THE UNION
THE MEMORY OF ABRAHAM LINCOLN
IS ENSHRINED FOREVER

The Lincoln Memorial in Washington, D.C., has become a symbol of the promise of America.

Timeline

AMERICAN HISTORY		WORLD HISTORY	
Native Americans of the Southwest begin farming.	**ca. 1500 BCE**	**ca. 2500 BCE**	The Egyptians build the pyramids and the Sphinx in Giza.
		ca. 563 BCE	The Buddha is born in India.
		313 CE	The Roman emperor Constantine legalizes Christianity.
		610	The Prophet Muhammad begins preaching a new religion called Islam.
		1054	The Eastern (Orthodox) and Western (Roman Catholic) Churches break apart.
Mississippian city of Cahokia reaches a population of more than 10,000.	**1100 CE**	**1095**	The Crusades begin.
		1215	King John seals the Magna Carta.
		1300s	The Renaissance begins in Italy.
		1347	The plague sweeps through Europe.
		1453	Ottoman Turks capture Constantinople, conquering the Byzantine Empire.
		1492	Columbus arrives in North America.
		1500s	Reformers break away from the Catholic Church, and Protestantism is born.
Spanish explorer Juan Ponce de León reaches Florida.	**1513**		
Spaniards bring the first enslaved Africans to what is now the United States.	**1526**		
Spaniards found St. Augustine, Florida, the first permanent European settlement in what is now the United States.	**1565**		
The first permanent English colony is founded in Jamestown, Virginia.	**1607**		
Plymouth, Massachusetts, is founded.	**1620**		
England controls eastern North America after the French and Indian War.	**1763**		
The American Revolution begins.	**1775**		
The Declaration of Independence is adopted.	**1776**	**1776**	The U.S. Declaration of Independence is signed.

AMERICAN HISTORY

The U.S. Constitution is drafted.	**1787**
George Washington is elected the nation's first president.	**1789**
The Louisiana Purchase doubles the size of the United States.	**1803**
The United States wins control of California and other southwestern lands from Mexico.	**1848**
The Civil War begins.	**1861**
The Civil War ends, and slavery is abolished.	**1865**
The United States enters World War I.	**1917**
The Nineteenth Amendment gives women the right to vote.	**1920**
The stock market crashes.	**1929**
President Franklin D. Roosevelt begins the New Deal.	**1933**
The United States enters World War II.	**1941**
Martin Luther King Jr. gives his "I Have a Dream" speech in Washington, D.C.	**1963**
U.S. ground troops arrive in Vietnam.	**1965**
President Richard Nixon resigns.	**1974**
Terrorists attack the United States, killing almost 3,000 people.	**2001**
The United States goes to war with Iraq.	**2003**
Hurricane Katrina destroys large sections of New Orleans, Louisiana.	**2005**
Barack Obama is the first African American elected president.	**2008**
Barack Obama is reelected president.	**2012**

WORLD HISTORY

1789	The French Revolution begins.
1865	The American Civil War ends.
1879	The first practical lightbulb is invented.
1914	World War I begins.
1917	The Bolshevik Revolution brings communism to Russia.
1929	A worldwide economic depression begins.
1939	World War II begins.
1945	World War II ends.
1969	Humans land on the Moon.
1975	The Vietnam War ends.
1989	The Berlin Wall is torn down as communism crumbles in Eastern Europe.
1991	The Soviet Union breaks into separate states.
2001	Terrorists attack the World Trade Center in New York City and the Pentagon near Washington, D.C.
2004	A tsunami in the Indian Ocean destroys coastlines in Africa, India, and Southeast Asia.
2008	The United States elects its first African American president.

Fast Facts

Official name: United States of America

Capital: Washington, D.C.

Official language: None

Washington, D.C.

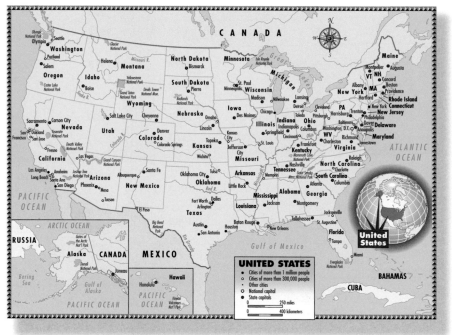

American flag

Official religion:	None
Year of founding:	1776, with adoption of Declaration of Independence on July 4
National anthem:	"The Star-Spangled Banner"
Government:	Federal republic
Head of state:	President
Head of government:	President
Area of country:	3,794,101 square miles (9,826,676 sq km)
Bordering countries:	Canada to the north and Mexico to the south
Highest elevation:	Denali (Mount McKinley), Alaska, 20,320 feet (6,194 m) above sea level
Lowest elevation:	Death Valley, California, 282 feet (86 m) below sea level
Longest river:	Missouri, 2,540 miles (4,088 km)
Largest lake:	Lake Superior, 31,700 square miles (82,100 sq km), shared with Canada
Average temperatures:	January, –7°F to 75°F (–22°C to 24°C); July, 45°F to 106°F (7°C to 41°C)
Average annual rainfall:	7.53 inches (19.1 cm) to 72.1 inches (183.1 cm)

Hawaii

New York City

Currency

National population (2010 est.):	315 million	
Population of major cities (2011 est.):	New York City, New York	8,244,910
	Los Angeles, California	3,819,702
	Chicago, Illinois	2,707,120
	Houston, Texas	2,145,146
	Philadelphia, Pennsylvania	1,536,471

Landmarks:
- ▶ *Badlands National Park*, Interior, South Dakota
- ▶ *Grand Canyon*, Arizona
- ▶ *Lincoln Memorial*, Washington, D.C.
- ▶ *National Air and Space Museum,* Washington, D.C.
- ▶ *Statue of Liberty*, New York City

Economy: The United States of America manufactures such large items as autos, electronics, and industrial equipment, as well as chemicals and food products. It exports raw materials, food, and finished goods to markets around the world. There is also a large service industry in the health, financial, communications, tourism, and retail fields. The United States is the world's second-largest producer of agricultural goods. Major products include corn, barley, oats, and soybeans. The nation also raises huge numbers of chickens and cattle.

Currency: The dollar.

System of weights and measures: Customary system

Literacy rate (2012): 99%

Student

Steve Jobs

Prominent Americans:

Hillary Clinton	(1947–)
First lady and secretary of state	
Ernest Hemingway	(1899–1961)
Nobel Prize–winning author	
Steve Jobs	(1955–2011)
Cofounder of Apple Inc.	
Martin Luther King Jr.	(1929–1968)
Civil rights leader	
Abraham Lincoln	(1809–1865)
President	
Toni Morrison	(1931–)
Nobel Prize–winning author	
Barack Obama	(1961–)
First African American president	
Georgia O'Keeffe	(1887–1986)
Painter	
Jackson Pollock	(1912–1956)
Painter	
Meryl Streep	(1949–)
Actor	
Mark Twain	(1835–1910)
Author	
George Washington	(1732–1799)
First president	

To Find Out More

Books

- Bjorklund, Ruth. *Immigration.* New York: Marshall Cavendish Benchmark, 2012.

- Blashfield, Jean F. *Slavery in America.* New York: Children's Press, 2012.

- Harasymiw, Mark. *Native Americans in Early America.* New York: Gareth Stevens Publishing, 2011.

- Marston, Daniel. *The American Revolutionary War.* New York: Rosen Publishing, 2011.

- McDaniel, Melissa. *The Industrial Revolution.* New York: Children's Press, 2012.

- Pinkney, Andrea Davis. *Hand in Hand: Ten Black Men Who Changed America.* New York: Disney/Jump at the Sun, 2012.

DVDs

- *The American Presidents.* Disney Educational Productions, 2010.

- *Artists Profiles: Musicians and Their Music.* Bennett Watt HD Productions, 2010.

- *Barack Obama.* A&E Television Networks, 2012.

- *How the States Got Their Shapes.* The History Channel, 2011.

▶ Visit this Scholastic Web site for more information
on the United States of America:
www.factsfornow.scholastic.com
Enter the keywords **United States of America**

Index

Page numbers in *italics*
indicate illustrations.

livestock, 78, 80–81
logging industry, 10
Long Beach, California, 85
Los Angeles, California, 23, 85, 85, 89, 101
Louisiana, 17, 30
Louisiana Purchase, 46
Ludington, Sybil, 44, 44

M

Maine, 14, 15, 27
manufacturing, 46–47, 51, 56, 79, 81–82, 83
maps. *See also* historical maps.
  geopolitical, 10
  population density, 88
  resources, 81
  topographical, 16
  Washington, D.C., 77
marine life, 27, 28, 29, 29, 30, 36
Maryland, 17, 40, 67, 77
Massachusetts, 39–40, 42, 43, 44, 120, 125
Massachusetts Bay Colony, 39–40
mastodons, 35
mayors, 76, 76
Mediterranean climate, 24
Melville, Herman, 111
Memphis, Tennessee, 60
Mexican-American War, 48
Mexico, 23
Michigan, 106
military, 32, 44, 45, 49–50, 51, 53, 54, 59, 60, 61, 62, 63, 64, 71, 72, 77
mining, 10, 48, 82, 83
Minneapolis, Minnesota, 24
Minnesota, 19, 24
Mississippi, 18, 89
Mississippian culture, 37, 37
Mississippi River, 18
Missouri, 20, 48
Missouri River, 16, 18

Mohawk people, 101, 101
Mojave Desert, 20
Monks Mound, 37, 37
Montana, 89
Mormonism, 100, 100
Mormon Tabernacle Choir, 100
Morrison, Toni, 112, 133
mounds, 37, 37
mountain lions, 28
Mount McKinley (Denali), 16
Mount Mitchell, 17
Mount St. Helens, 21
Mt. Waialeale, 16
museums, 77
music, 15, 23, 67, 100, 104, 113–115, 114, 115
Muslims. *See* Islamic religion.

N

National Aeronautics and Space Administration (NASA), 70
National Air and Space Museum, 77
national anthem, 67
national flag, 72, 72, 86
national holidays, 86, 123
National Museum of American History, 77
National Museum of the American Indian, 77
national parks, 50, 126
National Park Service, 126
National Science Foundation, 69–70
national seal, 87
Native Americans. *See also* people.
  agriculture, 35–36, 80
  ancestors of, 9
  Calusa, 37
  Cherokee, 93, 98, 98
  equality and, 60
  European exploration and, 38
  European settlers and, 11, 38, 39, 39, 40, 40

fur trade and, 39, 39
  Kateri Tekakwitha, 101, 101
  languages of, 94, 94, 95
  Mississippian culture, 37, 37
  Mohawk, 101, 101
  mounds, 37, 37
  music, 113
  National Museum of the American Indian, 77
  Navajo, 93
  petroglyphs, 105–106
  population of, 93
  Powhatan, 38
  religion of, 97–98, 98, 101, 101
  Taos Pueblo, 34
  Zuni, 38
Nebraska, 56, 75, 81
New Amsterdam colony, 38
New Deal programs, 55–56
New Jersey, 39, 89, 95
New Mexico, 34, 37, 90, 107
New Netherland colony, 38–39
newspapers, 42, 95, 111
New York, 19, 23, 23, 39, 42, 44, 89, 92, 125
New York City, 8, 23, 23, 25, 38, 44, 51–52, 53, 61, 61, 76, 89, 109, 127
New York Giants football team, 125
Nixon, Richard, 69, 69
North Carolina, 17, 17, 38, 41, 126
North Dakota, 89, 89
nuclear weapons, 57, 58–59, 62

O

oak (national tree), 32
Obama, Barack, 63, 63, 65, 71, 72, 133
Ohio, 110
oil industry, 10, 89
O'Keeffe, Georgia, 107, 107
Oklahoma, 93
Olmsted, Frederick Law, 109

Oregon, 20, 25, *26*
Orthodox Church, 101–102

P

Pacific Mountain System, 20–21
Parker, Charlie, *114*, 115
Patriots, 44
Peale, Charles Willson, 106
Pearl Harbor naval base, 57
Pei, I. M., 110
Pennsylvania, 43, 50, 61, 89, 106
Pentagon, 61
Pentecostals, 99
people. *See also* Native Americans.
    African Americans, 11, *11*, 37, 39,
        48, 51, 59, *59*, 63, 91–92, 112,
        114–115
    Asian Americans, 91, *92*, 93,
        102–103
    children, 47, *86*, 94, *94*, 95, *95*,
        106, 107, 119, *119*
    citizenship, 13, *13*, 48, 50, 68, 93
    education, 12, 75, 83, 94, *94*, 95,
        119–121, *119*, *120*
    ethnic groups, 90–93
    health care, 12, *75*, 84
    Hispanic Americans, 60, *74*, 87,
        90, *90*, 100, 114
    housing, 36, 37, *116*, 117–118
    immigrants, 8, 9, 11, 13, *13*, 23,
        47, 51–52, *53*, 79, 87–88, 91,
        93, *93*, 100, 102, 114, 125
    indentured servants, 41
    jobs, 12, *12*, 47, 52, 56, 81, 89, *89*,
        93, *93*
    languages, 40, 94–95, *94*, *95*
    Latino Americans, 60, *74*, 87, 90,
        90, 100, 114
    Pilgrims, 39, 40, 98
    population, 23, 88, *88*, 118
    Puritans, 39–40, 98, 99
    refugees, 88

segregation, 51, 59
slavery, 11, *11*, 39, 41, *41*, 45,
    48–49, 115
voting rights, 13, 51, 52, 59, 68
wealth of, 12
women, 47, 52, *56*
pesticides, 28
petroglyphs, 105–106
Philadelphia, Pennsylvania, 43, 89
Philippines, 53
Phoenix, Arizona, 89
Pikes Peak, 20, *20*
Pike, Zebulon, 20
Pilgrims, 39, 40, 98
plantations, 40–41
plateaus, 17
Platte River, 18
Pollock, Jackson, 107–108, 133
pollution, 33
Ponce de León, Juan, 37
population, 23, 88, *88*, 118
Potomac River, 77
Powhatan people, 38
presidents, 45, 49, 55, *55*, 58, *58*,
    60, 62, 63, *63*, *64*, 65, 68, 69, *69*,
    70–71, 72, *72*, 73, 77
Progressives, 52
Prospect Creek Camp, Alaska, 16
Protestantism, 52, 98–100
Providence, Rhode Island, 40
Puerto Rico, 53, 68
Puritans, 39–40, 98, 99

Q

al-Qaeda terrorist group, 61, *61*, 62
Quakers, 40

R

rabbits, 27
railroads, 10, 47, 52, 85, 118
Reagan, Ronald, 60
recipe (apple pie), 122, *122*

redwood trees, *26*, 27
refugees, 88
religion
    bar mitzvah ceremonies, *95*
    Buddhism, 97, 102–103
    Christianity, 96, 97, 98–100, *100*,
        100–102, *101*
    education and, 119
    Evangelicals, 99
    Greek Orthodox Church, 102
    Hinduism, 103
    Islam, 95, 97, 102
    Judaism, 39, 40, 95, *95*, 97, 102
    Mormonism, 100, *100*
    Native Americans, 37, 97–98, 101,
        101
    New Age, 103
    Orthodox Church, 101–102
    Pentecostals, 99
    Pilgrims, 39, 40, 98
    Protestantism, 52, 98–100
    Puritans, 39–40, 98, 99
    Quakers, 40
    Roman Catholicism, 40, 98,
        100–101, *101*
    Salt Lake Temple, 100, *100*
    shamans, 98
    Southern Baptist Church, 99
    United Methodist Church, 99
reptilian life, 30–31, *30*, *31*, 36
Republican Party, 76
Revere, Paul, 44
Rhode Island, 16, 40, 45
Rio Grande, 19
roadways, 75, 85, 119, *119*
Roaring Twenties, 54–55
Rocky Mountains, 19, 22, 25, 27, 32
Roman Catholicism, 40, 98, 100–101,
    101
Romney, Mitt, 100
Roosevelt, Franklin D., 55, *55*, 56, 80
roses (national flower), 32, *32*

Meet the Author

Michael Burgan has been writing for children for twenty-five years. He has written more than 250 books for young people, mostly about U.S. history and geography. He has written other titles in the Enchantment of the World series, including *Chile* and *Belgium*, and books about U.S. states for the America the Beautiful series published by Children's Press.

To prepare to the write *United States of America*, Burgan read many books on American history and other topics. He also did extensive research on the Internet, an essential tool for any writer today. Burgan says, "Perhaps the single most important source I turned to for up-to-date information was the U.S. Census Bureau, which has a huge amount of data online. Also helpful were sites run by the National Park Service and online versions of various magazines and newspapers, such as *Nature*, the *New York Times*, and *USA Today*."

Burgan enjoys traveling around the country, which has helped him learn more about the history and people of the United States. Having lived in three distinct parts of the country—New England, the Midwest, and now the Southwest—has added to his knowledge.

Apart from his nonfiction writing, Burgan also edits a newsletter for biographers called *The Biographer's Craft* and writes plays. Several of his plays have been performed around the country.

Photo Credits